Hollywood Speaks

Hollywood Speaks

Deafness and the Film
Entertainment Industry

John S. Schuchman

University of Illinois Press
Urbana and Chicago

Illini Books edition, 1999

© 1988 by the Board of Trustees of the University of Illinois
Manufactured in the United States of America
2 3 4 5 C P 5 4 3 2 1

∞ This book is printed on acid-free paper.

Library of Congress Cataloging-in-Publication Data

Schuchman, John S., 1938–
    Hollywood speaks.
    Filmography: p.
    Bibliographies.
    Includes indexes.
    1. Deaf in motion pictures. 2. Deaf—United States—
Social conditions. 3. Motion pictures—United States—
History. I. Title.
PN1995.9.D35S38   1988   791.43'09'0935208162   87-34287
ISBN 0-252-01526-6 (cloth : alk. paper)
ISBN 0-252-06850-5 (pbk. : alk. paper)

Digitally reprinted from the second cloth printing

Contents

Preface

When introduced to strangers, his father pointed a finger at his son, uttered a sound like "boy," and clasped an open hand to his chest in a possessive gesture. Then his father closed his hand in a fist, which represented the letter "s" in the manual alphabet, and tapped it lightly to the chin. Thus, the father introduced his son, Stanley.

The boy grew up in a household where he was the only person who could hear. His parents were deaf. Neither had understandable speech nor the ability to read lips very well. Although they could and did make vocal noises, they each communicated to their son and family friends through the use of American Sign Language.

Stanley lived within walking distance of most of his aunts and uncles, all of whom had emigrated to the United States before World War I. Among themselves, they preferred to speak Yiddish. None of them were deaf. Unlike his hearing cousins, Stanley's older relatives could not use signs and finger spelling. With his parents, they used a primitive system of gestures to communicate basic social information. If this failed, they called on the young boy to explain. Because of his parents' deafness, Stanley's family expected him to behave responsibly and often put him in charge of the other cousins. The parents, Florence and Harry, were always included in the affairs of the family.

In spite of this open and warm extended family circle, this was not where the deaf couple felt most comfortable. They sought out another circle: persons with whom they shared a language. Although these two circles of deaf friends and family knew each other and occasionally interacted at special events, such as Stanley's high school graduation and his mother's funeral, they represented two discrete worlds—hearing and deaf.

Outside of their house, Florence and Harry often communicated through simple gestures and facial expressions. Most evenings, Stanley's mother gossiped with her next-door neighbor through the exchange of written notes. Afterward, Florence carefully collected the notes and, in an air of shared confidentiality with her hearing neighbor, shredded the evidence of their innermost views of neighborhood events and personalities.

Deaf friends were spread throughout the city of Indianapolis. Although they knew deaf people all over the state, Stanley and his parents were particularly close with three other deaf families. On weekends, they traveled to these homes for card games or for a ride to events in the deaf community, as they did not have a car. All these deaf friends had children who could hear, like Stanley. Only one of the families had a telephone; the father of that family was really hard-of-hearing. If Florence or Harry needed a telephone, they sent Stanley with the message to a neighbor's house or to a nearby drugstore with a public pay phone.

Most of the deaf people Stanley knew were adults. During his childhood, he only knew one deaf child, Gilbert. Gilbert attended the local residential school for the deaf, and when he came home on weekends, Gilbert often visited Stanley's family. Although Gilbert had an older deaf brother, his parents did not use sign language. His elder deaf brother also visited Stanley's parents regularly. Most of Stanley's hearing playmates and cousins used individual signs and finger spelling to communicate with his parents.

The local movie theater was two blocks from Stanley's house, and his family attended regularly. Like other deaf families, they used the sign-language phrase "talk, talk, talk" to describe many of the movies they saw. This pejorative phrase meant that the film did not contain enough large action movements to enable a deaf person to follow the story. His parents occasionally asked Stanley to explain a particular action in the film but did not expect him to interpret the dialogue. His father usually fell asleep.

Television was not much better. Although not helpful to them personally, the deaf couple made the technology of sound available to their hearing son. They bought him a radio when he was a first grader. They were the second family on their block to purchase a television set. Other than the weather, most of the dialogue of television, particularly the evening news, was impossible for his parents to follow. Still, the television proved more serviceable than the radio. Baseball, wrestling, and "The Lone Ranger" were family favorites.

Stanley left for college in 1956. He took his radio with him. His parents tried to figure out the television news by themselves. By the time telecommunication devices, captioned films, and closed-captioned television came into popular use two decades later, his mother was dead and his father no longer interested.

This was my household and these were my parents.

Several years ago, Carol Padden, a linguist, developed useful definitions that distinguish "deaf culture" from the "deaf community." In essence, Padden defines the culture in a way that only includes individuals who have experienced deafness themselves. The deaf community, she maintains, is a broader group that includes persons who can hear and who share many of the values and goals of deaf people. I accept Padden's definitions, although doing so excludes me from deaf culture since I am not deaf.

I am, however, the only son of profoundly and prelingually non-speaking deaf parents who attended residential schools for the deaf and who used sign language at home. I grew up comfortable with sign language and communicated in signs and finger spelling without voice with my parents and our many deaf friends. Although my formal education consists of history and law, I have worked with and in behalf of deaf people most of my adult life. My surviving parent lives with me, and nearly twenty years of my professional life have been spent in the company of the students and faculty of Gallaudet University, a long-standing international institution of higher education in service to deaf people. Hence, I consider myself to be a member of the deaf community.

As for the movies, I make no special claim to cinematic expertise. However, the deaf characters I have seen on movie screens and on television bear little resemblance to the deaf people or community that I knew as a boy or that I know today as a professional in daily contact with deaf people. The purpose, then, of this book is to describe how Hollywood has depicted deaf characters over a period of more than eighty years and to compare this image with the deaf community as I understand it and have experienced it. It is my opinion that the film and television industries have dealt with deafness in a manner similar to their stereotyped treatment of ethnic and racial minorities. Thus, entertainment has been a substantial contributor to the public's general misunderstanding of deafness and to the perpetuation of attitudes that permit discrimination against deaf citizens. I have also prepared a formal filmography on deafness. When I started my research, none existed. My references represent the most complete compilation to date, and thus the filmography should be useful to others who wish to pursue further or allied research.

Many organizations and individuals have contributed resources and suggestions to this work. The National Endowment for the Humanities provided a summer stipend and travel grant; and Gallaudet University provided a sabbatical leave. The library and archives staffs of the Performing Arts Archive of Doheny Library at the University of Southern California; the Theater Arts Library and the Radio, Film, and Television Archives at the University of California, Los Angeles; the Margaret Herrick Library of the Academy of Motion Picture Arts and Sciences; the Louis B. Mayer Library of the American Film Institute; the California School for the Deaf at Fremont; the film departments of the Museum of Modern Art, George Eastman House, and the Museum of Broadcasting; the Film Archive and Manuscript Collection of the Wisconsin Center for Film and Theater Research; the M. C. Migel Library of the American Foundation for the Blind; the archives, library, and media collections of Gallaudet University; and the Motion Picture Division of the Library of Congress, all gave unstintingly of their resources and time to my requests for information and advice.

Mildred Albronda of San Francisco and Lisa Berke of Los Angeles shared information from their respective research on topics related to deafness and the arts. My wife, B. J. Schuchman, who is a faculty member at George Mason University, and my colleagues at Gallaudet University, especially Marin Allen, Anne Butler, Barry Crouch, Jack Gannon, Tom Harrington, and John Van Cleve, read various parts of the manuscript and filmography and made valuable suggestions. To each of these organizations and individuals I acknowledge my debt and express my appreciation. They shall remain blameless for any of the opinions and misstatements of fact that may remain; for these, I accept full responsibility.

Introduction

This is a book about motion picture films and television. The discussion also deals with the subjects of deafness and people who cannot hear. These two topics are interrelated because film media in the United States have represented an important source of public information about deafness and how deaf people relate to the larger society of persons who hear.

The products of Hollywood, both film and television, are evidence of a national cultural bias toward deafness and deaf people in the United States. For the most part, American movie and television viewers have never seen an active, healthy deaf community. Instead, consumers of the popular media depictions have been conditioned to see deaf persons as victims, usually dependent upon persons who hear. Even though filmmakers did not create these stereotypes, their popularization of derogatory and narrow depictions has contributed to the perpetuation of active discrimination throughout the twentieth century.

Many Americans have never met a deaf person. Even if one has, the opportunities for a dialogue often are frustrated because of communication barriers. In contrast to the experience of meeting a deaf person, most Americans have had an opportunity to see a deaf character depicted in a movie or television program. Since 1902, more than one hundred fifty movies and network television entertainment programs have included deaf characters and so have influenced our perceptions of deafness and deaf people.

Recent cultural and social scholarship dealing with issues of race, religion, ethnicity, and feminism has profited by the inclusion of film analysis in an effort to understand the milieu in which minorities and women interact with the majority American culture.[1] Unlike this growing body of scholarly literature, however, there is a comparative dearth of similar information about disability.[2] Yet there is little disagreement among writers on the subject of disability, many of whom are disabled themselves, that literary, film, and television images have been historically negative and stereotypical. Several observers have pointed out the traditional examples of Captains Ahab and Hook, as well as Richard III and Quasimodo, as evidence of the tendency of writers of literature and film to associate evil and malevolence with physical impairments and disfigurements.[3]

Many of these same commentators have stressed the importance of political activity by disabled individuals as consumers of media fare.[4] More directly, Paul Longmore has alleged that the recent film *Mask* (Universal, 1985), which depicts a positive image of a teenager with a rare facial disfigurement, reflects a "growing militancy in the disability community."[5] Some analysts have asserted that the increased number of disabled citizens, as a result of improved medical care and returning disabled Vietnam veterans, has resulted in more positive film images since the late 1970s. As proof, they typically identify such films as *Coming Home* (United Artists, 1978), *The Other Side of the Mountain* (Universal, 1975), and *The Deerhunter* (EMI Productions, 1978). It is too soon, however, to reach a general judgment about the film image of disability.[6] Along with detailed social science analysis, there is need for historical descriptions of the image of individual disabilities for both film and television.[7] To date, none exists.

In the United States, motion pictures and television represent and reflect a substantial part of the public image of the constituencies that make up American society and culture.[8] In times past, the able-bodied majority of Americans ignored the popular media views that stigmatized disabled citizens because films and television have accurately reflected and perpetuated the prevalent cultural perspective of disability, particularly deafness, as a pathological condition. Most Americans view deaf people as victims and as objects of pity. Even though they recognize the physical barriers that limit the access of disabled citizens, the notion that many of the problems of disabled citizens are rooted in our cultural views is not well understood.

Today, public policy, through legislation and judicial decisions, has moved in a direction that increasingly recognizes the goal of equality for disabled citizens. Like their other disabled brethren, deaf men and women are demanding that they have the right to be free of discrimination in the classroom, the workplace, and in public and state-sponsored forums. In their struggle for equal access and opportunity, deaf citizens have encountered apathy and ignorance in addition to discrimination by a general public oriented to sound and speech. As part of this struggle, it has been necessary to deal with and understand the public image of deafness. The literature of disabled citizens in general and deaf citizens in particular makes it clear that these groups consider films and television as their nemesis in the struggle for increased equality in the twentieth century.[9] Since discrimination operates in the context of cultural attitudes, it is crucial that the general public and filmmakers in particular understand the messages conveyed by America's most widely distributed cultural products: movies and television programs. In spite of increased sensitivity to the views and needs of disabled citizens in 1986, stereotypes and narrow depictions continue to predominate our viewing fare.

This study represents one historical description of a particular disability and the film entertainment industry. The deaf community is one of the oldest organized disability groups in the United States, and, as such, an analysis of the treatment of deafness by Hollywood filmmakers is an important link in understanding the evolution and persistence of discrimination against both disabled persons and minority groups in American society. Film, both motion pictures and television, represents a necessary source of documentation for the study of deaf people and deafness.[10] Although historians need to consider all sources of information about the past, film constitutes a particularly unique piece of evidence for a cultural or social analysis of the deaf community, since it is the only medium that can express the visual signed communication system of deaf individuals. However, like print documents, there are several types of film relevant to a study of deafness: (a) films of record, such as motion picture newsreels or television news broadcasts; (b) documentary films about deafness; (c) home movies from the deaf community; and (d) general entertainment films. While each of these sources is appropriate for study, this discussion will focus on the entertainment films of the motion picture and television industry (popularly known as Hollywood) because these are the documents that have the widest distribution and that best reflect the popular attitudes and cultural values of the general public.

The production of a film is a collaborative effort. A film's point of view must be endorsed broadly by the actors, editors, directors, producers, and writers who create it.[11] The so-called Hollywood point of view is a collective view of the teams of people who produce films.

Because the film industry is first and foremost a business, Hollywood survivors are those individuals who best can gauge what theater and television viewers find acceptable through box office receipts, criticism, and television ratings. Of course, an individual film may err, but a survey of films as a whole is a broad measure of popular attitudes and cultural values about a given subject.

In the past, most of the scholarship that has described deafness or deaf people has done so from a pathological point of view. From this perspective, a deaf person is defective, not normal, and so has required the medical, rehabilitative, or pedagogical assistance of professionals who are trained to deal with deafness as a disability, in common with other disabilities.[12] The pathological perspective also has dominated public policy in the form of legislation and judicial decisions affecting deaf people in the United States. However, since the late 1960s, an increasing number of scholars from such fields as anthropology, linguistics, and sociology have begun to document a cultural view of deafness that aligns deaf people with ethnic and linguistic minorities.[13] In fact, sociologist Paul Higgins has observed that deaf people only have difficulties when they are required to interact with the dominant culture of individuals who hear, or, as they are designated by deaf people, "hearing people." Although it is clear that most hearing people cannot or do not communicate easily with the few deaf persons they meet, they do have opinions about deaf people and deafness. Since Hollywood consists primarily of persons who hear, the product of Hollywood is a broad measure of these opinions of the hearing majority culture.

The silent film era represented the apogee of film viewing access for deaf people since it was the only time in the history of the industry that deaf individuals were comparatively equal members of the movie audience. Excluded from access in 1927–29, deaf citizens watched subtitled foreign films or guessed at the narrative of talking motion pictures for the next thirty years. By the 1960s, the federal government established a limited lending library of captioned movies for deaf viewers; most films remained uncaptioned. Those that were captioned usually became available to deaf viewers long after the initial release in the commercial theater market. In 1986, the industry had progressed to the point that Paramount Studios felt obliged to make a small number of captioned copies of the film *Children of a Lesser God* available for limited showings in major cities throughout the United States; in practice, this meant one copy per city for a short time. Paramount had no legal duty to make a film about deafness available to the deaf community, but in doing so it had the tacit support of the federal government. Conditioned to believe that it had no legal right to see such a film in a public theater, the deaf community did not complain very much even though deaf viewers could only see the captioned version in one theater and usually only at unpopular times.

Television was better. Early television was generally inaccessible, but in the 1970s, deaf consumers lobbied the national networks and the Federal Communications Commission to provide captioned programs. The networks rejected open captions as expensive and distracting to hearing viewers but agreed to support a newly perfected closed-captioned technology. In 1986, most prime-time television was available to deaf persons who had access to a television monitor equipped with a decoder able to receive the closed-captioned signal.

The image of deafness has also improved in recent decades. Many silent films used deafness as a trick: hearing men pretended to be deaf in order to capture a crook or an enemy. Otherwise, deaf characters were dependent victims, objects of pity or tragedy. In the first twenty years of talking pictures, filmmakers portrayed deaf characters as mutes, with no significant signed dialogue, or as naturally speaking heroes or heroines who read lips. *Johnny Belinda* (1948) represented the first major breakthrough for sign-language use in films. Thereafter, motion pictures and the newly popular television programs in the 1950s regularly featured deaf characters who used sign language in major roles. In contrast to their occasional appearances in the silent film era, no deaf actors played in a major film role until *Children of a Lesser God* in 1986. Television programming provided more, and earlier, opportunities. Yet in spite of the presence of deaf actors recently and an improved and sympathetic treatment of deaf characters, Hollywood scripts still have not acknowledged the existence of a deaf minority group in the United States.

The Deaf Community

In order to assess the Hollywood image of deafness, it is necessary to provide a brief history of the deaf community.[14] Although there is no exact census of the deaf, it has been estimated that there are approximately fourteen to sixteen million hearing-impaired persons in the

United States. Within this number, there are several groups who identify themselves as deaf and as part of the deaf community. Some
hearing-impaired persons choose not to be a part of the deaf community, particularly individuals who lost their hearing late in life. But for
those who choose to associate themselves with it, the deaf community
is an active and vigorous group that behaves very much like racial and
ethnic communities. Its antecedents go back to at least the early nineteenth century in the United States, and it has a close connection with
a much older French deaf community. The community came into existence out of a shared need to communicate and to deal collectively
with the majority culture of persons who hear. From its earliest days,
the deaf community understood that it would not be assimilated easily
into a culture dominated by the need to respond to sound and spoken
language. Among various groups of persons who possessed a physical
or sensory handicap, deaf persons were the first to develop an organized cultural response to the fact that the general society of hearing
people stigmatize deafness and deaf people as abnormal.

One of the best descriptions of the deaf community is contained in
sociologist Paul Higgins's *Outsiders in a Hearing World.*[15] Discussing
deafness from the theoretical perspective of deviance, Higgins points
out that "outsiders" often develop organizations to cope with the majority culture and that the deaf community is an example of such cop-
ing strategy. To be a member of the deaf community, it is necessary for
a deaf person to identify himself or herself as a deaf person, to experience deafness, and to participate in the affairs of the community.
Higgins, like most other commentators on the deaf community, has
observed that the symbol of membership in this community is not the
degree of hearing loss but knowledge of American Sign Language; and
the test of membership is an individual's acceptance and use of that
language. American Sign Language (ASL), or simply Sign, is not well
understood by persons who hear.

Sign is best understood when it is seen as one extreme of a language
continuum that is expressed manually.[16] At one end is a manual form
of the English language, the most precise form being finger spelling.
When this method is used, one simply spells on one's hand the letters
of an English word, phrase, or sentence. This approach, while precise,
is slow, tiresome, and requires accuracy as a speller of English words.
In lieu of finger spelling, one can substitute individual signs, such as
the sign for "chair," for the individual manual letters.

National Association of the Deaf, convention delegates, 1880. Deaf community leaders established the NAD to serve as a forum for the political and economic needs of deaf persons. Courtesy of Gallaudet University Archives.

THE FIRST DEAF FULL-LENGTH COLOR PRODUCTION
'DOG TROUBLE'

Starring

Marie Jansing
Chester Beers • Tippie

With Teresa Cikoch, A. Mangan, Hubert Shubert, Anita and Joe Greenberg,
Philip and Marie Burke, Virgil Owen, Mr. and Mrs. D. Luddy, Sally Miller,
T. Chabowski, Barbara and Madeleine Beers, Ernest Bardfeld, James Hunt,
Frank Bettencourt, Hugo and Dorothy Canaris, Theodore Woodruff, Mrs. C.
Sullivan, M. Reshatoff, Charles Wright, and Joe Massey.

•

A movie advertisement that appeared in the *Silent Cavalier* for *Dog Trouble* (1945), a sign-language film produced for the deaf community before the availability of closed-captioned television or captioned films. Courtesy of Gallaudet University Archives.

GEORGE W. VEDITZ, M.A.
PRESIDENT NATIONAL ASSOCIATION OF THE DEAF.

George Veditz (1861–1937), a teacher of the deaf and the seventh president of the NAD, led the effort to preserve sign language through the new medium of motion picture film prior to World War I. Courtesy of Gallaudet University Archives.

However, once a sign is introduced, ambiguity increases because most signs represent a concept, not an exact English word equivalent. For example, the sign for "chair" also represents the verb "sit" and the noun "seat." Certain combinations of finger spelling and signs are called Manual English because they adhere to English word order and rules of grammar. Some of these combinations provide for grammatical markers such as verb tense; others drop the markers. With all of these manual forms of English, deaf people have the option of adding whatever oral speech they may have (or moving their lips in approximation of spoken English). Moving toward the ASL extreme of the continuum, an individual would drop more of the markers of English grammar and the voice of spoken English. ASL itself, then, is a separate nonverbal language and does not depend on the rules of English or the voice.

Deaf persons tend to use ASL to communicate with other ASL users and to use various forms of Manual English to interact with hearing persons who know sign language. In fact, there are very few hearing persons who are competent users of ASL. Ignorant of its component parts, the general society of hearing persons refers to the entire continuum as sign language, whereas a deaf person quickly would recognize and categorize the communicator by the type of sign communication used. Hence, an ASL dialogue must be translated into English, no less than another language such as French, and is not merely a manual representation of English. Despite its visual orientation, ASL also is not pantomime. Since ASL is a language of the American deaf community, it is not understood by deaf people from other countries; however, since deaf people are more attuned visually, they will turn to pantomime and gesture to communicate with foreign deaf persons and hearing Americans, but only at a fairly simple level.[17]

From the deaf community's perspective, the use of ASL has been a traditional way to preserve and foster the interests of deaf people. For others, the use of ASL has marked deaf people as different and has represented the refusal of deaf people to assimilate themselves into the larger hearing culture. These others, often called oralists, maintain that deaf people should learn to speak orally and to read lips.[18] In response, deaf community members historically have argued that most pre-lingually and profoundly deafened people cannot speak intelligibly to the person on the street and that lip-reading is a very inexact art and impossible in group settings. When necessary for interaction with the hearing community, these deaf people prefer to use the Manual English forms of communication, written English notes, or an interpreter.

By the beginning of the twentieth century, and coincidentally with the beginnings of the film industry, oralists dominated residential schools for the deaf. The arguments of the oralists appealed to all groups advocating the importance of assimilation in the United States. The dependence of the deaf community on ASL was akin to the situation of ethnic communities and linguistic minorities. But, unlike ethnic communities, 90 percent of all deaf children have parents who hear— hence, sign language was not used at home and oralist teachers and administrators forbade its use in school. Oralists, who controlled the schools and the children, characterized this dispute over language as a pedagogical dispute, and argued that if deaf children were permitted to use sign language, they would become lazy and not learn to speak orally or to read lips. In contrast, the deaf adult community viewed the use of sign language as cultural. They referred to themselves as deaf people and understood that any attack on their language was an attack on their community, without which they would be isolated in a general hearing culture that refused to recognize the value and expressiveness of sign language.[19]

Building on the commonality of ASL, the deaf community has developed both local and national networks of organizations to meet the social and cultural needs of its members. In almost any large urban center or a site close to a residential or day-school program for deaf children in the United States, one will find a highly organized deaf community. For most of the twentieth century, this community has been tied together through the existence of a deaf club or association serving as the base for self-help social services and recreational needs. Several churches also have catered to the spiritual needs of deaf worshipers. The Episcopal church was one of the earliest and most active—particularly since it appointed ministers who were themselves deaf to serve the needs of these special congregations. And because deaf people encountered difficulty in obtaining insurance, they developed a voluntary insurance society in the early twentieth century. Each of these organizations, club, church, and insurance society, evolved their own social and recreational agendas, which were then reported in newspapers and magazines catering specifically to the local deaf community and to deaf individuals who lived at a distance from these centers. The newspapers alone stand as clear evidence of an active deaf community.

It is ironic that the deaf community, which identifies itself primarily through its members' use of ASL, is very much like most minority groups in the United States in its dependence on the printed word to communicate events and issues of importance.[20] The first known deaf editor of a newspaper was Evi S. Bachus, who acquired the *Canajoharie* (New York) *Radii* in 1837 and a few years later obtained money from the state legislature to mail the newspaper to "educated deaf people." Within a short time, many schools for the deaf published newspapers and the deaf press became known as the Little Paper Family.[21] At the turn of the century, *The Silent Worker* and the *Deaf-Mutes' Journal* both gained national status but were cut back to local school newspapers with the onset of the Great Depression. After their demise, several newspapers of the deaf were established throughout the United States. One in particular, the *Silent Cavalier,* stood apart from the rest in that it was independent of schools for the deaf as well as organizations of the adult deaf.[22] The *Cavalier* began as a state publication in the early 1940s, but within a short period of time it made the transition to national prominence and for a decade was at the center of most issues dear to the deaf population. The deaf community perceived the *Cavalier* and its editors as advocates in their behalf at a time when the National Association of the Deaf did not see advocacy and lobbying as its legitimate functions.

Historically, deaf people had neither a legal right nor convenient access to the services of interpreters. Until the second half of the twentieth century, deaf citizens of the United States depended upon the goodwill of their hearing children, friends, relatives, churchworkers, and residential school personnel to voluntarily interpret for them the spoken English of the hearing world in which they resided and worked. By the 1960s, groups of interpreters and deaf consumers recognized that in order to establish interpreting as a legally recognized service for deaf clients, there was a need to develop interpreting as a field of study and as a profession. In 1964 a national organization for interpreters was created, which became the Registry of Interpreters for the Deaf. This new organization quickly established standards for the evaluation and training of interpreters and, most important, championed the passage of local and state laws that provided interpreting services for deaf individuals.[23] Robert Weitbrecht's invention in 1964 of an acoustic coupler that permitted a telephone signal to be converted and transmitted as a teletypewritten message was also a significant development of this period.[24] The telephone, which had become a basic medium of communication in an increasingly urbanized America and which was once an impossibility for people who could not hear, was now accessible to the deaf community. By the end of the 1960s, organizations representing the entire spectrum of hearing-impaired persons—from oralists to those who use sign language—cooperated in forming Teletypewriters for the Deaf, Inc., a national organization that maintains a directory, monitors telecommunication issues, and encourages widespread adoption of the device among the deaf community as well as the public and private institutions that deal with deaf persons.

The need to develop captioning technology became more pressing as the movie and television industries continued to expand. As with the acoustic coupler inventor, Weitbrecht, deaf individuals tried to find ways around the technology of sound. Silent film actor Emerson Romero had devised a cumbersome technique of adding captions between film frames, which obstructed the flow of the story, and his efforts to develop a national film library did not meet much success either. Even more difficult was the problem of how to obtain rights to various films from the studios; and later this included gaining access to television. In the fifties, Edmund Boatner, headmaster of the American School for the Deaf, established a not-for-profit corporation to caption films for deaf viewers but soon realized that a national distribution system was financially prohibitive. He convinced the federal government to establish a national lending library of film for deaf viewers, via Public Law 85–905 (September 1958), which expanded throughout the 1960s.[25]

It is ironic that, at the same time the federal government was dismantling "separate but equal" institutions in response to racial issues, it was advocating "separate but equal" treatment for the deaf community in terms of entertainment and educational film viewing. One can make a strong case that this was a legally "reasonable" solution to the problems of a so-called special population, yet it fell far short of the hoped-for requirement that the entertainment industry, engaged as it was in interstate commerce, provide captions for all movies and television programs that enter the marketplace.[26] Given the absence of political clout and the magnitude of the resources required to convince the federal government and the industry to do otherwise, the deaf community had no choice but to accept what was offered. However, it was not long before deaf community leaders began to adopt the language and strategies of political and civil rights advocates. But before deaf awareness and advocacy activities could succeed, the chief deaf representative organization needed to change and the research findings produced by scholars of deafness needed to be translated for the general public. The National Association of the Deaf (NAD) and the National Theatre of the Deaf (NTD) took on these roles.

At its twenty-seventh convention in 1964, the NAD renamed its national publication (formerly *The Silent Worker*) the *Deaf American*. The members also approved the establishment of a new home office in Washington, D.C., and two years later the NAD hired its first full-time executive secretary, Frederick C. Schreiber. Building on many of the early accomplishments of the NAD under the presidency of Byron B. Burnes, Schreiber moved to develop the home office into a modern and professional consumer advocacy organization. He developed contacts throughout the federal bureaucracy and the Congress which enabled the NAD to receive government contracts and to become a major force in behalf of deaf persons.[27] An important symbol of this progress was the Deaf Olympics, properly known as the World Games for the Deaf, which took place in the United States in 1965. The Games originated in France in 1924, and American deaf athletes had participated since 1935. Now, in contrast to many sports organizations for the deaf in other countries which were funded by their governments and managed by hearing individuals, the American deaf sports community, with the support of the NAD, insisted that it manage and operate the Games, utilizing the facilities of Gallaudet College and the nearby University of Maryland.[28]

With the increased visibility and assertiveness of the deaf community came a push for identification with the performing arts. Earlier, in 1934, deaf actors in New York City responded to the comparative absence of entertainment options for the deaf by establishing the Theatre Guild.[29] Most cities with sizable deaf populations followed suit; for example, the Chicago Silent Dramatic Club began annual performances in 1937 that included skits and vaudeville as well as major dramatic plays.[30] In New York, deaf actor Ernest Marshall utilized an interest in photography and film—as well as connections with former silent film actor Emerson Romero—to produce nine feature films between 1937 and 1963, each of which consisted of an all-deaf company

performing either an original script by a deaf writer or an adaptation
of a classic.[31] Then, in 1965, the National Theatre of the Deaf came
into existence at the Eugene O'Neill Theater Center in Waterford, Connecticut.[32] Two years later, this mixed company of deaf and hearing
actors performed before a national television audience and thereafter
in cities throughout the United States.

Under the leadership of a successful Broadway scenic designer, David Hays, and an experienced deaf actor—mime, Bernard Bragg, the
NTD consciously aimed to change popular attitudes toward deaf people
and deafness through performances that emphasized the communicative richness and beauty of sign language.[33] Hearing actors spoke and
signed their lines and interpreted the sign-mime dialogue of their fellow deaf actors, enabling mixed audiences of hearing and deaf patrons
to understand the entire performance. Even though a federal grant
served as the catalyst for the emergence of the new repertory company,
in actuality the NTD was the result of the persistence of deaf actors in
the practice of their craft for most of the twentieth century despite the
general unwillingness of professional film, television, and theater companies to hire them. Without public or professional support, the actors
had worked evenings and weekends, often without pay, for their special audiences. Now, the full-time deaf actors of the NTD could devote
their creative energies to sharing the identity and experiences of the
deaf community with audiences everywhere. Although there was little
change in Hollywood films, the NTD was successful in theater and
television.

There are deaf people who are single, lonely individuals, just as there
are hearing people who are single, lonely, and uncommunicative.
There are deaf people who speak well and are excellent lip-readers,
but in most instances they are individuals who lost their hearing late
and who already had a good command of spoken English or who have
residual hearing and benefit from the use of hearing-aid technology.
Sometimes, these deaf people reject sign language and interaction with
other deaf adults. There are some deaf people who are illiterate and do
not know sign language. But the average deaf person uses some form
of sign language and participates to some degree in the affairs of the
deaf community. These same individuals have neighbors and co-
workers who can hear and interact with them through written notes or
some form of Manual English. If married, the deaf individual is prob-

ably married to another deaf individual, and chances are that their children, if they have any, can hear.[34] It is this average deaf person and his or her community of choice that has not been accurately depicted by the motion picture and television entertainment industry.

In many ways, the earliest era of Hollywood's history was the most important for the deaf community because silent films represented an important opportunity for the mainstream of American society to embrace deaf people. When Hollywood excluded deaf persons from participation in and access to what had become, in the eyes of the world, one of our most important cultural products, the act of exclusion represented a societal failure to provide deaf people with the promise of equality contained in the Declaration of Independence.

NOTES

1. Examples in the past decade are: Sarah B. Cohen, ed., *From Hester Street to Hollywood: The Jewish-American Stage and Screen* (Bloomington: Indiana University Press, 1986); Thomas Cripps, *Slow Fade to Black: The Negro in American Film, 1900–1942* (London: Oxford University Press, 1977); Molly Haskell, *From Reverence to Rape: The Treatment of Women in the Movies* (New York: Penguin Books, 1974); Randall M. Miller, *The Kaleidoscopic Lens: How Hollywood Views Ethnic Groups* (Englewood, N.J.: Jerome Ozer Publisher, 1980); and James R. Nesteby, *Black Images in American Films, 1896–1954: The Interplay between Civil Rights and Film Culture* (Washington, D.C.: University Press of America, 1982).

2. A recent issue, "Media Depictions," of the *Disability Studies Quarterly* makes it clear that several scholars are interested in this subject. See Paul K. Longmore, "Talking Back to the Media," *Disability Studies Quarterly* (Summer 1986), pp. 1–2. For the first extensive filmography of a disability, see Wendy Erickson and Diane Wolfe, comps., *Images of Blind and Visually Impaired People in the Movies, 1913–1985: An Annotated Filmography with Notes* (New York: American Foundation for the Blind, 1985).

3. See Leonard Kriegel, "Claiming the Self: The Cripple as American Male," in *Disabled People as Second Class Citizens*, ed. Myron G. Eisenberg et al. (New York: Springer Publishing, 1982), pp. 52–63; Paul K. Longmore, "Screening Stereotypes: Images of Disabled People," *Social Policy* (Summer 1985), pp. 31–37; S. Thurer, "Disability and Monstrosity: A Look at Literary Distortions of Handicapping Conditions," in *Rehabilitating People with Disabilities into the Mainstream*, ed. A. D. Spiegel and S. Podair (Park Ridge, N.J.: Noyes Medical Publications, 1981), pp. 51–57.

4. Cynthia Griggins, "The Disabled Face a Schizophrenic Society," in *Disabled People as Second Class Citizens,* pp. 30–39.

5. Paul K. Longmore, "'Mask': A Revealing Portrayal of the Disabled," *Los Angeles Times Sunday Calendar* (May 5, 1985), pp. 22–23.

6. Myron G. Eisenberg, "Introduction," in *Disabled People as Second Class Citizens,* pp. xiii–xvii; Sonny Kleinfield, *The Hidden Minority: A Profile of Handicapped Americans* (Boston: Little, Brown, 1977), pp. 25–33.

7. The American Foundation for the Blind filmography (see n. 2) identifies more than two hundred depictions of visual impairment in the movies. Paul Longmore (see n. 5) has identified more than a thousand disabled characters on film and television (Longmore to Schuchman, personal correspondence, August 18, 1986).

8. For a general discussion of film and American culture, see Garth Jowett, *Film: The Democratic Art* (Boston: Little, Brown, 1976); Gerald Mast, *A Short History of the Movies,* 2d ed. (Indianapolis: Bobbs-Merrill, 1976); Lary May, *Screening Out the Past: The Birth of Mass Culture and the Motion Picture Industry* (New York: Oxford University Press, 1980); Leonard Quart and Albert Auster, *American Film and Society since 1945* (New York: Praeger, 1984).

9. For an excellent introduction to the perspective of disabled groups, see Frank Bowe, *Handicapping America: Barriers to Disabled People* (New York: Harper & Row, 1978).

10. For an introduction to the study and bibliography of film and history, see Peter C. Rollins, "Film, Television, and American Studies," in *Hollywood as Historian: American Film in a Cultural Context,* ed. Peter C. Rollins (Lexington: University of Kentucky Press, 1983), pp. 246–71.

11. William Hughes, "The Evaluation of Film as Evidence," in *The Historian and Film,* ed. Paul Smith (Cambridge: Cambridge University Press, 1976), pp. 67–73.

12. Psychologist Harlan Lane has described the early history and European origins of this pathological and medical view of deafness in *When the Mind Hears: A History of the Deaf* (New York: Random House, 1984); see also Harlan Lane, ed., *The Deaf Experience: Classics in Language and Education,* trans. Franklin Phillip (Cambridge: Harvard University Press, 1984), pp. 2–12.

13. For example, see Carol Erting, "Language Policy and Deaf Ethnicity," *Sign Language Studies* (1978), pp. 139–52; James Woodward, *How You Gonna Get to Heaven If You Can't Talk with Jesus: On Depathologizing Deafness* (Silver Spring, Md.: TJ Publishers, 1982). These and other scholars built on the linguistic first steps of William C. Stokoe, an English professor at Gallaudet College, who worked in the 1960s to describe the structure of the "visual communication" system used by deaf people. This included publica-

tion of *A Dictionary of American Sign Language*, rev. ed. (Silver Spring, Md.: Linstock Press, 1976), in which he and his colleagues made it clear that sign language is not a pidgin or "dumb" version of English but a language with its own syntax and rules of grammar.

14. Although dated, a standard description is Jerome D. Schein and Marcus Delk, *The Deaf Population in the United States* (Silver Spring, Md.: National Association of the Deaf, 1974).

15. Paul C. Higgins, *Outsiders in a Hearing World: A Sociology of Deafness* (Beverly Hills, Calif.: Sage Publications, 1980).

16. A brief survey of sign language and finger spelling appears in Lottie L. Riekehof, *The Joy of Signing* (Springfield, Mo.: Gospel Publishing, 1978), pp. 4–14.

17. However, the World Federation of the Deaf has sponsored the development of standard signs, used primarily at international meetings. See Unification of Signs Commission, World Federation of the Deaf, *Gestuno: International Sign Language of the Deaf* (Carlisle, England: British Deaf Association, 1975).

18. Although many deaf people who use sign language also use their voices and read lips, oralists oppose the use of signs, particularly with and among children. The Alexander Graham Bell Association for the Deaf (AGB), located in Washington, D.C., is the national organization of oralists. Although the organization, membership, and administration are overwhelmingly dominated by persons who hear, there is a small group of oral deaf adults. As of 1975, there were less than three hundred oral adult deaf members of AGB. See *Oral Deaf Adults Handbook* (Washington, D.C.: Alexander Graham Bell Association for the Deaf, 1975).

19. For a current statement of a deaf person's perspective, see Leo Jacobs, *A Deaf Adult Speaks Out*, 2d ed. (Washington, D.C.: Gallaudet College Press, 1980).

20. See Lubomyr and Anna Wynar, *Encyclopedic Dictionary of Ethnic Newspapers and Periodicals in the United States*, 2d ed. (Littleton, Colo.: Libraries Unlimited, 1976), p. 14.

21. For a description of the deaf press, see Jack R. Gannon, *Deaf Heritage: A Narrative History of Deaf America* (Silver Spring, Md.: National Association of the Deaf, 1981), pp. 237–51.

22. The *Cavalier* is equally interesting because it came into existence as a result of an oral-manual controversy. See Reuben Altizer to John Schuchman, Happy Hands Club Oral History Interviews, Videotaped Interview, July 1981, Gallaudet University Archives, Washington, D.C. (hereafter, GU Archives); Altizer to Schuchman, Cavalier Project Interviews, Videotaped Interview, September 1983, GU Archives. See also the *Virginia Guide*, a publication of the Virginia School for the Deaf and Blind (Staunton, Va.),

particularly the issues dated January 15, 1930; March 15, 1930; May 1931; November 1931; February 1932; May 1932; March 1935; January 1936; May 1939; June 1939.

23. For a general description of the 1960s and the deaf community, see Gannon, *Deaf Heritage*, pp. 317–56.

24. In addition to Weitbrecht's invention of the acoustic coupler, there are many other telecommunication devices which deaf people use. For a description and discussion, see Jerome Schein and Ronald N. Hamilton, *Impact, 1980: Telecommunication and Deafness* (Silver Spring, Md.: National Association of the Deaf, 1980).

25. Any group of six deaf individuals can establish a club and thereby receive entertainment films from the national lending library. Similarly, educational films are widely distributed throughout the nation to programs for deaf children. See Emerson Romero's comments on "The National Film Library for the Deaf," *The Silent Worker* (January 1951), p. 23. For a more general description, see Gannon, *Deaf Heritage*, pp. 266–69.

26. For an excellent description of the technology and terminology of captioning, as well as the pros and cons of interpreting for television, see Schein and Hamilton, *Impact, 1980*.

27. For a discussion of Schreiber's work for the NAD, see Jerome Schein, *A Rose for Tomorrow: Biography of Frederick C. Schreiber* (Silver Spring, Md.: National Association of the Deaf, 1981).

28. For an introduction to the scope of sports activities in the deaf community, see Gannon, *Deaf Heritage*, pp. 271–316.

29. See "Theatre Guild," *Deaf-Mutes' Journal* (August 1934), p. 4.

30. For a brief description of the Chicago group, see "Spotlight," *The Frat* (March 1952), p. 2.

31. Ernest Marshall to John Schuchman, Videotaped Interview, October 1981, GU Archives; see also the Marshall Scrapbook, GU Archives. Marshall's film list includes *It Is Too Late* (1937), *The Debt* (1955), *The Confession* (1956), *The Face on the Barroom Floor* (1959), *Ten Barrooms in One Night* (1961), *The Neighbor* (1961), *Sorrowful Approach* (1962), and *A Cake of Soap* (1963). Although the original films remain in Marshall's possession, he has allowed some of them to be copied by Gallaudet University and shown on campus. Other deaf filmmakers of Marshall's era included Chester Beers of California, Alexander McDade of Ohio, and Clyde Cherrington of Michigan; however, none of their films are known to exist.

32. See Bert Shaposka, "The Origin and Concept of the Proposed National Repertory Theater of the Deaf," *Deaf American* (May 1967), p. 7.

33. Hayes and Bragg have been incredibly successful. For twenty years the NTD has regularly toured throughout the United States and abroad. Most deaf actors working today in television and film are former members of the

NTD (Marlee Matlin, who won an Academy Award for her performance in *Children of a Lesser God*, is an exception). Although it is impossible to prove, the company's tours appear to have whetted the national appetite for sign-language classes and information about deafness. In addition to performances, the NTD also conducts educational programs and workshops that afford deaf performers the opportunity to work with established actors, writers, and directors.

34. A recent publication describes a deaf family from the perspective of their hearing daughter: Lou Ann Walker, *A Loss for Words: The Story of Deafness in a Family* (New York: Harper & Row, 1986).

1

The Silent Movie Era

A historical analysis of the early motion picture industry and the deaf community clearly illustrates the importance of movies to an understanding of the social and cultural history of deafness and deaf people in the United States.[1] These were years in which deaf people perceived themselves and their language, American Sign Language (ASL), to be under attack from the so-called oralists. Influenced at the end of the nineteenth century by theories of assimilation and eugenics, public policy began to turn against the deaf community, which did not speak English, married among its own members, and maintained separate institutions. At an 1880 international meeting in Milan, Italy, a convention of mostly European educators of deaf children passed resolutions that advocated "the oral method [over] that of signs in the education and instruction of deaf-mutes."[2] The European position provided moral support to like-minded American educators, and the Milan conference became a pejorative symbol of oralism within that part of the deaf community that used sign language. With public champions such as Alexander Graham Bell and Helen Keller, oralists deposed sign language as well as deaf teachers and administrators from the residential school curriculum and hierarchy. In 1911, the state of Nebraska enacted the first oral education law, which required the state school for the deaf to use oral methods in lieu of finger spelling and sign language in the belief that its deaf citizens would thereby be integrated into the mainstream of society. Deaf leaders railed against these events, but to little avail.[3]

One part of the strategy by the national deaf leadership, in response to these attacks, was to make use of the new motion picture technology. Very quickly they understood that film was a medium that could express the language of the deaf community, which heretofore had been impossible. Recognizing the decrease in the number of deaf teachers available to teach signs to schoolchildren, the National Association of the Deaf (NAD) established and funded a project to film and thereby preserve sign language for the future. Between 1910 and 1921, more than a dozen such films were produced. Using a technique comparable to commercial films of the day, filmmakers worked with 35-mm film and a stationary camera to record a collection of poems, lectures, and memories signed by men and women who were considered to be master storytellers and signers. By 1927, these films had been exhibited throughout the deaf community: in twenty-nine cities, at twenty-seven conventions, and in fifty-six schools for deaf students.[4]

The history of the early film industry reveals that the silent film era inadvertently included deaf people to an extent unknown today. Deaf people participated in the industry as equal members of an audience, as pedagogical beneficiaries at school, as actors on the screen, and as subjects for film scripts. Representative comments of contemporary editorial writers and columnists of *The Silent Worker,* one of the major publications of the deaf community press,[5] reflected the interest in movies:

> We deaf people must thank the screen-art for the one biggest offset to our infirmity. Good pictures, and by good pictures I mean the kind that educate and elevate, are the levers that lift us from the deadly dullness and monotony of total deafness, to the highest pinnacles of delight.[6]

> Most deaf people are movie fans, and while the present generation probably reads far less than their predecessors, they are as well informed, and they are broader by reason of what they have learned from the movies.[7]

> The deaf are more dependent upon the movies for their entertainment and instruction than any other class of people. Against their wills, they and their children have been fed the trashiest material; more trashy than dime novels could ever be. Much of it is vile. . . . The people do not want too many high brow, educational films, but they do want good, wholesome and clean scenes.[8]

The deaf community saw the many advantages of motion pictures. During the early silent years of film, deaf persons sat in movie house audiences everywhere in the United States and participated, on a comparatively equal basis, with their hearing peers, as dramas, comedies, and the news unfolded on the theater screen. Interpreters, special captions, headsets, or other assistive devices were unnecessary. From the perspective of today's sensitivity to physical and sensory handicaps, silent films represented a golden era of equal access for deaf individuals to the most democratic form of public entertainment of that time. Unfortunately, Hollywood had not planned to accommodate deaf viewers—it had just happened. Hence, when the technology of films developed a voice in 1927–29, the industry saw no need to make any special provision for audiences unable to hear the new "talkies."

As talking motion pictures captured the movie market, the superintendents of schools for the deaf were one of the first groups to organize in an effort to convince movie producers that captioned films were necessary. Residential schools had made use of motion pictures from the earliest days, for both education and entertainment. For example, in the spring of 1915, the New Jersey School for the Deaf had scheduled a moving picture series on Thursday evenings for students to see reels about San Francisco, nature study, mining, book making, and the production of straw hats and rope. Via the Hearst-Selig News Pictorial, deaf children saw a German cruiser, a tango demonstration, as well as war news; for entertainment, they saw the two-reel comedy *The Moving Picture Cowboy*.[9] More than a dozen state schools for the deaf had "expensive cinematograph machines." [10]

Teachers of deaf students understood the educational value of these films. Articles that discussed movies often appeared in the *American Annals of the Deaf*, the professional journal for American educators of deaf children.[11] Persons who are unfamiliar with silent films might assume that it was the English captions that made them valuable for English language–deprived deaf children, but this was not so. Although captions helped, it was the silent films' visual orientation that made them so beneficial, particularly the use of facial expression and body movement.[12] The best silent films tried to tell their stories without words, and when they succeeded, they provided a substantial base of information from which a teacher could develop a transition to English for deaf children, many of whom could not read captions or the actors' lips. This is why artists like Charlie Chaplin, who used very little lip movement, were such favorites with deaf viewers.

In the late 1920s, the peak of the silents, movies served as the substantive content for deaf student work in the form of letters, journals, and essay contests. In 1926, students at one of the largest residential schools, the Indiana School for the Deaf, saw films at chapel on

Wednesday nights and Thursday mornings. For a nickel, "to defray the cost of these pictures which are the same as are shown in the best downtown theatres," they could see entertainment films on Saturday mornings. Taking advantage of this opportunity, the school sponsored an essay contest in which students wrote on the topic of what movies could teach.[13] In the same year, half of the fourteen student letters that appeared in *The California News* school section dealt with several movies the students had seen on their own in the San Francisco area.[14]

There is little disagreement among educators of deaf children that the handicap of deafness is primarily a communication disorder that often results in low English achievement. It was particularly unfortunate, then, that the potential of English-language development identified by teachers and deaf writers in the silent movie era did not have an opportunity to be further nurtured. Schools struggled on without this resource, and the Great Depression and intervening wars resulted in other national priorities. The federal government now subsidizes some captioning for deaf viewers, but it is clear that the demise of the silent film represented an educational tragedy for deaf children. It also effectively ended the careers of five deaf actors who had appeared in silent films, two of them consistently in supporting roles and the others primarily as extras with occasional small parts.

The deaf actors were Granville Redmond, Emerson Romero (stage name Tommy Albert), Albert Ballin, Louis Weinberg (stage name David Marvel), and Carmen de Arcos. Unlike other actors, such as Louise Dresser, who may have been deafened in later life but were culturally hearing individuals, these deaf actors had attended schools for the deaf, knew sign language, and were accepted by other profoundly deaf persons as deaf. Of these five, Redmond was the one most often described in publications for the deaf, and most of these referred to his relationship with Charlie Chaplin. In fact, when independent film producer James Spearing showed his all-deaf movie *His Busy Hour* to deaf audiences in order to obtain funds for distribution,[15] one of the reasons given for lack of financial support from the deaf community was the failure to include Redmond as a member of the cast. It was pointed out that he had proven his ability to act with "big-time stars" like Chaplin, Douglas Fairbanks, and Raymond Griffith.[16]

Redmond studied art at the residential school for the deaf at Berkeley, California, and later in Paris. He achieved recognition as a landscape artist and became a permanent fixture in San Francisco art circles.[17] In 1917, Redmond played the role of a "colored cook" in a yacht film, produced by a San Francisco film company, which was shown "on the curtain of the Bohemian Club," of which he was a member.[18] Contemporaries commented that he was clever in the "art of mimickry," and his skill apparently brought him to the attention of Chaplin, who then invited him to Hollywood. Alice Terry, a prominent leader in the California deaf community and a neighbor of the Redmonds, reported that Redmond had misgivings about the movies since he did not use his voice; but Chaplin had assured him that it was not necessary to speak, that "plain ordinary lip movements will do."[19] Chaplin also gave Redmond space to paint at the Chaplin production facilities, where Redmond produced some works for films, others for himself, and some that Chaplin purchased. Although there is no direct evidence from Chaplin about his interest in the deaf actor, Redmond spoke favorably of his employer. In a 1919 letter to T. H. D'Estrella, his former teacher at the California School for the Deaf, Redmond referred to work on the film *A Day's Pleasure* and the fact that the company had been idle. However, he pointed out that Chaplin allowed him to paint at the studio and that he was happy because "he [Chaplin] is able both to make himself understood and to understand me. He is an artist."[20] Others confirmed Redmond's view.

In his autobiography, *It Took Nine Tailors* (1948), Adolphe Menjou, who appears in Chaplin's *Woman of Paris* (1923), and in a group photograph that includes both Chaplin and Redmond, said that Chaplin enjoyed having creative artists around him and used an example of a painter who worked on the lot to buttress his point. Although Menjou did not mention Redmond by name, nor did he mention the painter's deafness, Redmond appears in the group photograph with Menjou, wearing an artist's smock.[21] Other writers alleged that Chaplin escaped to Redmond's studio where he could enjoy the paintings and the quiet: "When Chaplin wants to rest he goes where he is sure that he will get it—away from the fuss and babble of human tongues—directly to the quarters of his peaceful deaf-mute friend."[22] Deaf artist and sometime actor Albert Ballin interviewed Redmond at the studio and reported that "on the opposite side was a setee, in which a little slender man was seated. My host scribbled something on his 'conversation' pad and made a gesture of introduction: 'Mr. Charles Chaplin'."[23] All of this occurred in the early twenties, approximately five years after Redmond appeared in his first Chaplin film, *A Dog's Life,* in 1918. In short, it

Charlie Chaplin *(right)* executing the letter "d" in the manual alphabet with deaf actor Granville Redmond *(left)*. Both actors appear in costume on the set of *A Dog's Life* (First National, 1918). Courtesy of Gallaudet University Archives.

Deaf actor Granville Redmond, as the dance-hall manager, ejects the tramp, the dog, and Edna Purviance in this scene from *A Dog's Life*. Courtesy of Gallaudet University Archives.

Deaf actor Albert Ballin as the hermit in the all-deaf-cast film *His Busy Hour,* produced by James Spearing in 1926 but not distributed. Courtesy of Gallaudet University Archives.

Albert Ballin, deaf actor and author. Courtesy of Gallaudet University Archives.

Deaf entertainer Louis Weinberg (stage name David Marvel) performed as a vaudeville dancer and in the silent film *The Woman God Forgot* (Artcraft-Paramount, 1917). Courtesy of Gallaudet University Archives.

Deaf actor Emerson Romero (stage name Tommie Albert), in costume for *Henpecked in Morocco* (ca. 1926). Courtesy of Gallaudet University Archives.

(Top): Emerson Romero and his wife, Emma, after his forced retirement from silent motion pictures. Romero actively pursued film captioning technology and deaf theater repertory productions. *(Bottom):* On a return to Hollywood, Romero, with his wife and daughter, visits his cousin, the actor Cesar Romero. Courtesy of Emma Romero.

Deaf actor Granville Redmond *(center)*, in artist's smock, on the set of *A Woman of Paris* (United Artists, 1923), with Charlie Chaplin and Adolphe Menjou *(third and fourth on the left)*. Courtesy of Gallaudet University Archives.

seems that Chaplin respected Redmond's painting, enjoyed the sense of quiet, and could afford to subsidize Redmond's presence on the movie lot.

In addition to his role as Edna Purviance's boss, the dance hall manager in *A Dog's Life,* Redmond appears in at least four, and possibly five, other Chaplin films: *A Day's Pleasure* (1919), *Sunnyside* (1919), *The Kid* (1921), *A Woman of Paris* (1923), and *City Lights* (United Artists, 1931).[24] In *The Kid,* he is in an early scene as the artist friend of the kid's natural father. In *A Woman of Paris,* Redmond plays the role of a guest at a wild party in a Paris apartment, where he tries to break up a drunken brawl. Although a well-built man, distinguished looking, with a head of white hair and occasionally a mustache, he is not readily recognized in *A Day's Pleasure* or in *Sunnyside,* even though he identified himself or received credit as a member of both casts.

Redmond's role in *City Lights* reflects the dilemma of the deaf actor. The opening scene depicts the unveiling of a park statue, in whose lap Chaplin's "little tramp" character has taken refuge, under the canvas. As the platform party is introduced to the crowd in this well-advertised pantomime challenge to the new talkies, a microphone stands as a reminder of noise, and Chaplin uses an unpleasant sound, literally "blah-blah," to represent the speech of the host and emcee. One of two dignitaries who is introduced to the crowd is played by Redmond, and although there is no direct evidence that Chaplin chose a deaf actor who would be oblivious to the noise of the dedication, the fact remains that Redmond is there. Unfortunately, even if the symbolism were deliberate, it ends as a private joke since the audience was not privy to the fact that the actor was deaf.[25]

Aside from these roles and an apparent general friendship, there is no direct evidence that Chaplin acquired any nonverbal communication skills or techniques from Redmond.[26] Chaplin was quite successful long before the two met; however, the deaf community early identified Chaplin as being deaf or at least having deaf relatives in order to explain his facility to communicate with movie audiences with little or no lip movement. In fact, when Helen Keller was in Hollywood for the production of her own biographical film, *Deliverance* (1919), she and her teacher-companion Anne Sullivan Macy visited the Chaplin studio. Publicity photographs show Keller finger spelling to Chaplin, and the captions indicate that she taught him to finger spell.[27] Since

other photographs, which appeared in *The Silent Worker,* also assert
that Redmond taught Chaplin finger spelling, these episodes can be
attributed to the desire for publicity for particular films.

Redmond appeared in other movies, including *The Three Muske-
teers* (1921), with Douglas Fairbanks, and *He's a Prince* (1925) and
You'd Be Surprised (1926), with the popular comedian Raymond Griffith. Of these, his most important role was in *You'd Be Surprised,* in
which he plays a deputy coroner who pretends to be a deaf butler and
communicates in signs and finger spelling with the film's star, Griffith.
Except for a few cameo appearances, this is the only known or surviving Hollywood film in which a deaf actor plays a deaf adult character
(albeit, a fake deaf person), until the present day. Apparently ignorant
of Redmond's deafness, and failing to mention his name or even list it
in the film credits, a *New York Times* film reviewer observed that "one
of the humorous notions in this piece of work is the introduction of a
deaf and dumb valet, with whom the coroner [Griffith] is able to communicate by signs." [28] As an actor, then, Redmond received scant recognition outside of the deaf community; as a painter, his landscapes
still attract attention. [29]

When his silent film career ended in 1927, Emerson Romero returned to New York City where he married and became active in the
deaf community. Although none of his films are known to exist, subsequent interviews and photographs reveal that he played comedy roles
from 1925 through 1927 in such films as *Beachnuts, The Cat's Meow,
Great Guns,* and *Sappy Days.* Copyright registrations indicate that
Mack Sennet, Bobbie Vernon Comedies, and the Christie Comedy
Films produced movies with these titles.

A native of Cuba, Romero received his education at the Wright Oral
School in New York City. He returned to Havana to work with his
brother for the Pan American Picture Corporation, where he developed
his comedic skills in such films as *La Chica del Gato.* A visiting Hollywood producer, Richard Harlan, saw Romero's work and invited him
to California. In a 1927 interview, the only contemporary account of
how he, as a deaf actor, functioned on the set, Romero reported that
he would read the lips of the director and then establish his timing
before the cameraman shot the actual film footage. He also mentioned
the only known deaf actress of the period, Carmen de Arcos. Romero
explained that "she is mute too, having never been to an oral school.
However, she is very clever with signs." [30] Although he identified de

Arcos as his leading lady, contemporary photographs of her were from Spanish-captioned films, making it doubtful that she appeared in American films with Romero.

Romero made use of his professional skills when he returned to the East Coast. Although he earned his living in other ways, he became active in deaf theater groups and became known as a master storyteller and performer for deaf audiences. He helped organize a deaf theater group, directed and advised the making of movies with all-deaf casts for the deaf community, and pioneered in efforts to superimpose captions on commercial films, thereby making Hollywood films accessible, once again, to deaf people. It was these latter-day activities for which he has been remembered in the deaf community. In recent interviews, contemporaries noted his theatrical and captioning efforts and the fact that his first cousin is the popular film star Cesar Romero, but no one remembered any of this deaf actor's films.[31]

Another professional deaf entertainer was David Marvel. Born Louis Weinberg, he was educated at the Lexington School for the Deaf in New York City. One of several deaf dancers, Weinberg developed a vaudeville act; contemporaries described him as a "famous Russian toe-dancer." He made a film appearance as one of many Indian princes in *The Woman God Forgot* (1917), starring the opera diva Geraldine Farrar.[32] Thereafter, he remained on the vaudeville circuit with no further film appearances.

Albert Ballin was the only other deaf person to appear in films. In many ways Ballin was the most thoughtful, since he was the only one who wrote about deafness and films, perhaps because he was never successful at acting. Although "my being a deaf-mute has never been considered an obstacle," he asserted, his film experience consisted primarily of $7.50/day stints as an extra. He wrote that he usually was lost in the crowd but alleged that he was easily recognized in *Silk Stockings* [*Silk Legs* (?)] (Fox, 1927), *The Man Who Laughs* (Universal International, 1927), *Michigan Kid* (Universal International, 1928), and *The Woman Disputes* [*Disputed* (?)] (United Artists, 1928).[33] Ballin did secure a role in *His Busy Hour* (Heustis, 1926), but the movie with an all-deaf cast was never distributed commercially and remains lost, as does the cast list.

Supporting himself as a writer, lithographer, photographer, and portrait painter, Ballin wrote a script, *Sardanapolus,* which he sold to the Palmer Photoplay Corporation, hoping that it would be made into a movie. He moved to Hollywood in 1924 and, through his friendship with J. Parker Reed, Jr., a business manager for the successful movie producer Thomas Ince, gained access to the studios. For several months, Ballin was hired and fired from jobs as a photo retoucher, but he managed to survive as a portrait painter. At the William Fox Studios, he painted the portrait of Tom Mix's three-year-old daughter, Thomasina, which led to other Hollywood commissions. Ballin appeared to be one of those marvelous individuals who easily made friends with the famous and near-famous. In his writing, he referred to detailed conversations with Alexander Graham Bell, Lon Chaney, Charlie Chaplin, and Betty Compson; and when he staged a benefit to publish his book, Ballin managed to convince such "stars" as Laura LaPlante and Neil Hamilton to appear on the dais to speak in his behalf.

Ballin's book, *The Deaf Mute Howls* (1930), which has been described as one of the first publications written by a deaf person to rage against the oralist domination of deaf education and deaf people, contains several themes. One section deals with Ballin's view that a working knowledge of sign language could help actors and the movies. Using Lon Chaney as an example, Ballin argued that sign language develops nonverbal communication skills such as facial expression and body movement. He also contended that sign language would be a beneficial means of communication on noisy film sets and proposed that there be sign language films as an alternative to silents and talkies. No one took him up on the idea and Ballin was never heard from again.[34]

Nor were any of the other deaf actors.[35] Except for Redmond's cameo appearance in *City Lights,* talking motion pictures cut short the promising careers of this small group, and the notion that deaf persons might be natural actors was never given an opportunity to develop in Hollywood. Thereafter, deaf actors such as Emerson Romero persisted in the practice of their trade throughout the United States in local deaf theater groups, performing before their own special audience, the deaf community. Forty years later, this persistence would be rewarded with the creation of the National Theatre of the Deaf, a repertory company.

The silent movie era may have been beneficial to the deaf community in terms of physical access, but because, with one exception, deaf actors did not play roles as deaf characters, they had little or no opportunity to influence the popular image of deafness as portrayed in silent films. Hollywood contributed to the stereotype of deaf people as deaf and dumb or as dummies whose deafness was transmitted genetically. Hearing aids, ear trumpets, and sign language itself were transformed into visual gimmicks designed to elicit laughter, and it became common for characters to feign deafness in order to catch or trick a villain. When the silent movies occasionally pitted deafness against blindness, the deaf character was most often cantankerous and ill humored, in contrast to the peaceful, serene, visually impaired character. Deaf characters were invariably lonely, alienated from society, and sometimes, in despair, contemplated suicide. Unfortunately, these stereotypical images survived the demise of the silent films and continued to perpetuate misinformation and false images of deaf people and their emotions to the American public. Since most hearing persons rarely encountered a deaf person, the movies exerted a powerful negative influence comparable to similar derogatory film stereotypes experienced by American blacks, Indians, women, and ethnic groups.

It is possible to put together a fairly accurate account of the image presented to movie audiences through an examination of extant films, photo stills, copyright registrations, scripts, publicity press kits, and comments in columns and letters to the editors of publications from the deaf community. Over a comparatively brief silent film era, more than a dozen films depicted a central or pivotal character who was deaf or who feigned deafness. In 1902, the American Mutoscope and Biograph Company produced *Deaf Mute Girl Reciting "Star Spangled Banner."* Like most motion pictures of its day, and as implied by the title, the film had no story line; it was simply a recitation of the national anthem. Because of the novelty of motion picture technology, the early movies served to "record" daily life, which in this case included sign language. This film, which has been reconstructed from the paper print collection of the Library of Congress, depicts a young woman who performs an accurate platform ASL rendition with an American flag in the background. Unfortunately, there are no captions; hence, an audience unfamiliar with sign language would not be able to appreciate the power and beauty of this visual performance. Later, as films with narrative plots were popularized, hearing actors, like their white counterparts in blackface, played the roles of deaf characters in stereotyped forms.

The Dummy

Despite the absence of any anatomical connection between the larynx and an individual's auditory senses, filmmakers persisted in linking an inability to hear and to speak: *The Deaf Mute* (1913), *The Silent Voice* (1915), *Menace of the Mute* (1916), *The Dummy* (1917), *The Silent Stranger* (1924), and *Deaf, Dumb, and Daffy* (1924). The term "deaf and dumb" had been quite common in deaf education prior to the twentieth century, but due to the pejorative use of "dummy," it became increasingly unacceptable to the deaf community—something the movie industry ignored. In its synopsis of *The Dumb Bandit* (Rex, 1916) for theater owners, the trade newspaper *Moving Picture World* actually equated the term "dummy" with sign language when it explained that "the bandit pulls his gun, tells the wife *in dumb* he is going to kill. . . ."[36]

Most unexpectedly, the "dummy" label also appears in the film *Deliverance* (Helen Keller Film Corp., 1919), which depicts the life of Helen Keller. Closed off from speaking engagements on the Chautauqua and Lyceum lecture circuits by the advent of World War I, the thirty-seven-year-old Keller explored other forums for her moral and social beliefs, as well as an opportunity to earn a livelihood for her companions and herself.[37] Francis Trevelyan Miller, editor of a popular photographic history of the Civil War, convinced her that a film would be an excellent vehicle; that a film would allow her to reach the thousands of moviegoers who did not attend lectures. Privately financed by industrialist Charles Schwab, the world-famous deaf-blind spokesperson and her equally famous teacher-companion, Anne Sullivan Macy, traveled west to make the motion picture—a captioned photo-biography of Keller's life. Although the film did not provide the financial returns nor future security she and others had hoped for—"It seems strange to me now that I ever had the conceit to go the long, long way to Hollywood, review my life on the screen, and expect the public not to fall asleep over it."[38]—film reviewers gave it positive marks and commented on the spontaneous applause of audiences. One viewer, Harry Weber, invited Keller to perform on the vaudeville stage, which she did for four years, until she retired from the entertainment circuit to devote her energies full time to the American Foundation for the Blind.[39]

Although Keller advocated several social and moral causes during this period of her life, one of her constant messages in public appearances was that "the deaf and the deaf-blind can and must be taught to speak." This is made clear in her film, though racial stereotypes are used to draw a negative connection between the term "dumb" and intelligence. After scenes that portray her birth and the subsequent discovery of her handicap, the captions read: "Blind—Deaf—and Dumb!!"; ". . . a lonely wild animal without knowledge—without thought. . . ." Taking advantage of Keller's southern upbringing and early life in Alabama, in a later scene a stereotyped pickaninny sees her stumbling about and says: "De debbil's suttinly got dot chile!" Still later, Keller tries to teach her dog the manual alphabet and the same little black girl pities her and observes: "She can't never know nothing . . . or be smart like us." Later, Keller takes speech lessons and, turning to the audience, says via captions, *"I—am—not—dumb—now."* The film shows her teachers crying, and contemporary film reviews reported that the audiences cried too.[40] There is no question that Helen Keller was sincerely and absolutely convinced of the importance of speech, but there also is no question that scenes such as these made the unfortunate and erroneous point in the public's mind that persons who did not speak were mentally inferior—especially to a movie audience which had no opportunity to ask questions.

The Fake Deaf Person

In the public mind, there was a connection between handicaps, begging, and fakes. To distance itself from this popular misconception, the National Association of the Deaf adopted the slogan "The deaf do not beg." No silent film portrayed a deaf beggar or peddler, but several films depicted hearing characters who feigned deafness. Two films that included fake handicaps starred Lon Chaney, who in real life was the son of deaf parents.

In one of his most famous films, *The Hunchback of Notre Dame* (Universal, 1923), Chaney plays the deafened hunchbacked bellringer, Quasimodo. One of the central characters in the film is Clopin, the king of the Paris thieves, whose hideout is the Court of Miracles, where the fake blind and crippled beggars truly see and walk. Although the film's virtue is that Quasimodo is good and rescues the gypsy dancer, Esmeralda, the film still reinforces the image of the disabled as fakes. This theme is central to the plot of one of Chaney's early films, *The Miracle Man* (Artcraft/Paramount, 1919), in which a gang uses a deaf-mute, the Patriarch, who is losing his sight, as a bogus faith healer to bilk unsuspecting contributors. Chaney has the role of Frog, a fake cripple who, as a part of his act, is cured and dramatically unwinds his twisted body. Much to the surprise of the gang, a little crippled boy is inspired by the deaf-mute Patriarch and actually *is* cured. The gang decides to go straight, "and when the Patriarch passes on he leaves four mended lives—who . . . have been made over into wholesome, healthy human beings by the power of suggestion he so unconsciously exerted on them."

Many of the fakes in these early movies are the so-called good guys. *Martyrs of the Alamo* (Fine Arts, 1915) features the legendary character and namesake of a Texas county, Erastmus "Deaf" Smith, renamed Silent Smith in the film, who served as a spy and scout for Sam Houston during the Texas war for independence. In the film version, Smith feigns deafness in order to gather intelligence from the enemy, led by the Mexican general Santa Anna. When the Mexican troops speak to him, Smith makes the sign for deaf (a touch of the finger first to the ear, then to the mouth) and shakes his head "no," indicating that he cannot hear; suspicious, one of Santa Anna's officers fires a rifle behind Smith, to which he fails to respond. Convinced that he is deaf, the Mexicans proceed to discuss their plans in his presence, as Smith faces the camera and slowly smiles in the knowledge of his successful ruse. Thereafter he rescues his sweetheart, escapes, and returns to General Houston to join in the battle of San Jacinto. Masquerading as an ordinary captured soldier, Santa Anna is surprised when he meets Smith, who obviously can hear and identifies him as the Mexican leader.

Three other films of this type, *The Dummy* (Paramount, 1917), *The Silent Stranger* (R-C Pictures, 1924), and *You'd Be Surprised* (Paramount, 1926), depict hearing characters who fake deafness in order to catch crooks. Although the objective is perhaps laudatory, the portrayal once again reinforces the commonly held view that handicapped persons often are fakes trying to obtain money through pity.

In *The Dummy*, based on a popular stage play of the same name by Harvey O'Higgins and Harriet Ford, Jack Pickford stars as Barney, a

The Miracle Man (Paramount, 1919). Joseph Dowling *(right)* as the Patriarch, a deaf-blind faith healer who cures Frog, a fake cripple played by Lon Chaney *(left)*. Courtesy of the Wisconsin Center for Film and Theater Research.

Deliverance (Helen Keller Film, 1919). Etna Ross *(center)* as the young Helen Keller. Courtesy of the Wisconsin Center for Film and Theater Research.

Voice in the Dark (Goldwyn, 1921). A deaf patient, played by Gertrude Norman *(seated)*, mistakenly identifies a murder suspect. Courtesy of the Wisconsin Center for Film and Theater Research.

The Dummy (Paramount, 1917). Jack Pickford played a young detective who fakes deafness to capture kidnappers. Courtesy of the Wisconsin Center for Film and Theater Research.

young detective who claims he "can hold his tongue and talk deaf and dumb." Barney is hired to imitate a "wealthy deaf and dumb boy" in order to be kidnapped by a gang that has already taken a young girl. The stratagem works as Barney fools the kidnappers and rescues the young girl.

The Silent Stranger represents the western version of this fake genre, in which a secret service agent (played by Fred Thompson), aided by his horse, Silver King, fakes deafness in a successful investigation of thefts of U.S. mail. Trade newspaper advertisements depicted the "deaf" agent with a gag tied across his mouth.

The most interesting of these three films is *You'd Be Surprised,* starring comedian Raymond Griffith as a coroner investigating the murder of the owner of a missing diamond necklace. After he has interrogated the partygoers at the murder scene, Griffith discovers an eyewitness, a deaf-mute valet, played by Granville Redmond. Although Redmond signs that he is deaf, in order to test him, the coroner snaps his fingers behind Redmond's ear; getting no response, he fires a pistol behind the valet and again gets no response.[41] Convinced that he truly is deaf, the coroner finger spells, "I speak your language," which appears as a caption on the screen. Excited at meeting someone with whom he can converse, the deaf valet proceeds to tell what he has seen.

In a later scene, the deaf valet recounts his story for the coroner's jury. Suddenly the lights go out. When they are turned back on, Redmond is stretched out on the floor with a knife in his back. The coroner continues his investigation and soon confronts the murderer, who asks for the missing evidence, a man's shirt cuff with an incriminating thumbprint on it. Griffith blows a whistle and the so-called dead deaf valet appears, mouthing the words "Did you call me chief?" which appear as a caption on the screen. He gives the cuff to the coroner, thereby sealing the murderer's fate, and everyone (including the audience) is surprised to discover that the valet can hear and is in fact a deputy coroner. Griffith jokingly finger spells something to Redmond, who laughs and leaves. What seems to have escaped the film reviewers, who commented favorably on this device, was that Redmond was really deaf.[42] No deaf contemporaries criticized him publicly for playing this stereotyped role; on the contrary, deaf people were proud of his achievement, as evidenced by publications within the deaf community which consistently praised his work as an actor.

The Deaf Person as an Object of Humor

Deafness sometimes provided opportunities for humor, and hearing aids and ear trumpets were easy targets in the early movies. In *An Italian Straw Hat* (Albatross/Sequana, 1927), a deaf uncle's ear trumpet is stuffed with material, making him oblivious to the fights and general chaos that occur behind his back. In *You'd Be Surprised,* manual communication itself is a source of humor. Throughout the film, however, Redmond appears as a dignified deaf valet, and he always signs or finger spells appropriately. As the deputy coroner, he laughs when Griffith finger spells to him, and it is clear that he is laughing at the successful deception.

In this film signs provide two types of humor: captions and visual gags. The captions take advantage of the fact that the audience does not know the actual content of the dialogue between Redmond and Griffith. For example, Griffith finger spells, "What know," to which Redmond responds by pointing to an opening in the ceiling and sign-miming that he opened a trapdoor and looked down. He then finger spells, "I saw it." Griffith looks pleased. The audience reads the following caption: "He saw everything from the skylight—and wore out three fingers yelling for help."[43] In a subsequent scene, Griffith builds a visual gag using the fact that finger spelling allows one to "talk" with one's mouth full. Assembling a coroner's jury of assorted characters, including a hot dog vendor and a milkman, he asks Redmond to testify about the position of each of the suspects at the murder scene. As the coroner finger spells uncaptioned questions, he buys a bottle of milk, which he drinks, continuing his finger spelling with his right hand; he adds a hot dog, with mustard and sauerkraut, which he stuffs into his mouth, "talking" all the while. The visual gag is finally broken up with a fight.

The Unhappy Deaf Person

Invariably, deafness as represented in films means loneliness and despair. Based on a play of the same title, *The Silent Voice* (Quality Productions, 1915), and its subsequent retitled version, *The Man Who Played God* (United Artists, 1922), tell the story of a concert pianist who loses his hearing. In despair, he attempts suicide but is saved by friends who urge him to learn to lip-read, which then becomes the vehicle for his salvation. In *Seige* (Universal, 1925), a deaf character is ridiculed by family and friends when he shows affection for one of his female relatives. Alone and depressed, he commits suicide.

Being alone is also the norm for deaf persons in the movies. During the silent movie era, no film depicted more than one deaf character; those who were married or had sweethearts were linked always with a member of the opposite sex who could hear. A few films took advantage of this to portray such relationships as based on pity (*The Silent Voice* and *The Man Who Played God*) or deception (the two previously named films and *Bits of Life* [Marshall Neilan Productions, 1921]). Probably the most blatant example of an unhappy deaf character appears in *A Voice in the Dark* (Goldwyn, 1921), which contrasts deafness with blindness. Two characters, a deaf woman and a blind man, patients in a sanatorium, "see" and "hear" a murder. The prime suspect, accused on the basis of what the deaf character saw, is freed when the blind character correctly identifies the murderer on the basis of what he heard. The screen credits identify the deaf character, Mrs. Maria Lyiard, played by Gertrude Norman, as "deaf, and with an irritable disposition," in contrast to the blind character, played by Alec Francis, who is "sightless, but still loving life and nature."

The only happy deaf character in a silent film turns out to be naive. In episode two, subtitled "Man Who Heard Everything," of the film *Bits of Life*, "Ed Johnson [is] deaf, but he [is] happy in the belief that his wife love[s] him . . . and his belief that the whole world is good." A good samaritan gives Johnson, who is a barber, a device that restores his hearing, and he soon discovers that his hearing wife has taken advantage of him and has been unfaithful, and that his closest friends are corrupt. "Instead of being a blessing, the instrument has changed the whole world from one of joy to one of despair. With a stone he smashe[s] the device." This film is intriguing because another episode starred the increasingly popular character actor Lon Chaney, whose own deaf father was, in fact, a barber.

The Expert Deaf Lip-reader

Two films, *The Silent Voice* and *The Man Who Played God*, dealt directly with lip-reading. In both, the deafened hero learns to lip-read in an incredibly short period of time and with the aid of binoculars reads the lips of people sitting on a park bench below his penthouse apartment. Wealthy from his days as a musician, he decides "to play God" and through financial assistance solves the problems he reads about on the lips of the people below him. He gradually regains his faith in God and also discovers that his wife is truly faithful to him, in spite of his suspicions to the contrary. At film's end, he strikes his head and regains his hearing.

Indirectly, silent films contributed to the lore of lip-reading when both the national and the deaf community presses reported on the detection of obscene utterances by screen actors. In 1911, the Board of National Moving Picture Film Censors appointed Irene Langford to monitor the movies for obscenities. The board took note of the fact that some actors used "bad language . . . which can be seen and understood by deaf and dumb people who understand spoken words by reading the lips."[44] In spite of the reference to the purported skills of deaf moviegoers, the board's appointee, Ms. Langford, could hear. Regrettably, there was no distinction drawn between an ability to lip-read a single- or multi-word obscenity and an ability to lip-read whole sentences and conversations.

When the movie industry converted to the new sound technology in 1927–29, such publicity adversely affected deaf viewers, as most hearing persons believed that deaf people generally were expert lip-readers. In spite of the concerted efforts of the Conference of Superintendents and Principals of American Schools for the Deaf, oral deaf and hard-of-hearing clubs, and various other deaf groups, Hollywood ignored requests to provide captioned versions of the new talkies. Elwood Stevenson, superintendent of the California School for the Deaf in Berkeley, spoke for all of these hearing-impaired groups when he wrote that "it is practically impossible for even expert lipreaders to follow the talking pictures under the best of conditions."[45] Not only did the industry ignore the testimony of such prominent educators as Stevenson, in 1932 it proceeded to remake *The Man Who Played God* as one of the new talking pictures, thus strengthening and perpetuating the stereotyped ability of deaf people to read lips.

The silent movie era was contradictory in its overall effect upon the deaf community. Deaf leaders, as well as persons who worked with and in behalf of deaf people, understood the powerful potential of motion pictures to benefit deaf people. Well before the close of World War I, motion pictures had become a regular part of life, in and out of the classroom, at most residential schools for the deaf in the United States. However, it was the technology of motion pictures, which for the first time permitted the visual language of deaf people to be preserved, that most intrigued the deaf leadership. Now, the image and culture of deafness could be shared. In its film project, the NAD had hoped that the symbol of the deaf community, sign language, would be preserved. In a moving speech, the NAD president, George W. Veditz, explained the importance of film to deaf people:

> Fifty years from now, these moving pictures will be priceless. We must, with these various films protect and pass on our beautiful signs as we have them now.
>
> As long as we have deaf people on earth we will have signs, and as long as we have our films, we can preserve our beautiful sign language in its original purity.
>
> It is my hope that we all will love and guard our beautiful sign language as the noblest gift God has given to deaf people.[46]

These sentiments were not understood in Hollywood. Instead, commercial films depicted deafness and deaf people in the same way that they dealt with other minority groups—through prevalent, and thereby reinforcing, stereotyped views. The negative and misleading images that appeared on theater screens in the silent movie era persisted for the next half century. The greatest tragedy came in 1927–29, however, when the industry converted to the new technology of talking motion pictures, thereby bringing to a close the most positive aspect of the silent film era for the deaf community—equal access.

NOTES

1. For an earlier analysis, see John S. Schuchman, "Silent Movies and the Deaf Community," *Journal of Popular Culture* 17:4 (Spring 1984), pp. 58–78.

2. For a discussion of the convention, see Edward L. Scouten, *Turning Points in the Education of Deaf People* (Danville, Ill.: Interstate Printers, 1984), pp. 195–205.

3. John Van Cleve, "Nebraska's Oral Law of 1911 and the Deaf Community," *Nebraska History* 65 (Summer 1984), pp. 195–220.

4. See Roy J. Stewart, "Motion Picture Fund Report, NAD Convention Proceedings," *The Silent Worker* (July 1927), pp. 371- 73. When the dangers of nitrate-based film became apparent, the NAD arranged to have the films

converted to 16-mm safety film, and copies were donated to Gallaudet College and to the Library of Congress.

5. Since the printing trade offered excellent employment opportunities for deaf male graduates of this era, nearly all schools published a newspaper, and many of the vocational instructors in the printing department were themselves deaf. The papers' editors established a communication network, and the school newspapers came to be known as the Little Paper Family. During the silent movie era, two publications stood out: *The Silent Worker*, produced at the New Jersey School for the Deaf, and the *Deaf-Mutes' Journal*, produced at the New York School for the Deaf (Fanwood) . These became the de facto national publications of the deaf community. For a summary and description of publications from the deaf community, see Jack R. Gannon, *Deaf Heritage: A Narrative History of Deaf America* (Silver Spring, Md.: National Association of the Deaf, 1981), pp. 237–51.

6. *The Silent Worker* 32 (October 1919), p. 20.

7. Ibid., 33 (March 1921), p. 195.

8. Ibid., 33 (May 1921), p. 280.

9. "School and City," *Silent Worker* 27 (January 1915), p. 71.

10. Ibid., 27 (May 1915), p. 154. Since the writer overlooked his own school, this must be taken as a conservative count.

11. For example, see Lucile M. Moore, "The Deaf Child and the Motion Picture," *American Annals of the Deaf* 63 (November 1918), pp. 467–75.

12. Silent film audiences routinely spoke of good "acting" or its absence. For a discussion of the importance of facial expression and body movement, see Kevin Brownlow, *The Parade's Gone By* . . . (New York: Ballantine Books, 1968), pp. 344–53.

13. "Movie Essays," *Silent Hoosier* 39 (September 1926), pp. 1, 7.

14. "Student Letters, Miss Nourse's Class," *California News* 40 (April 1926), pp. 126–27.

15. Spearing, formerly a *New York Times* movie editor, met some deaf people in 1918 and, with financial backing from Bertha Lincoln Heustis, produced *His Busy Hour.* With the help of a pantomime teacher, Gabrielle Ravenelle, he recruited an all-deaf cast, but since the filmmaker intended the movie for general audiences, there was no attempt to use sign language. (See "Deaf Mutes Perform in Motion Pictures," *New York Times* [December 12, 1926], VIII, 7: 1.) Even though Spearing was a professional scriptwriter who worked at the Paramount Studios on Long Island and in Hollywood, he was unable to secure funds for distribution of the two-reel comedy, a project that served as a practical test for the often stated notion that deaf people were natural actors. The movie was shown to a deaf audience at the Lexington School for the Deaf in New York in order to create interest in forming an all-deaf film company, but in 1926 the deaf community was not interested. (See

Albert Pach, "With the Silent Workers," *The Silent Worker* 39 [December 1926], pp. 59, 62.) The deaf community believed that their equal access to films and the occasional employment of deaf actors like Redmond and Romero did not require a special deaf film company. Three years later, the deaf community was one of the few groups that wanted the silents to continue and, indeed, might have benefited from a deaf movie company.

16. Pach, "With the Silent Workers."

17. Art historian Mildred Albronda, who has written previously on the deaf artists Douglas Tilden and T. H. D'Estrella, is currently writing a monograph on Redmond's career as an artist.

18. *California News* 33 (November 1917), p. 48.

19. Alice Terry, "Moving Pictures and the Deaf," *The Silent Worker* 30 (June 1918), p. 154.

20. *California News* 34 (September 1918), pp. 112–13. A contemporary newspaperman confirmed the ability of the two men to communicate easily. See the *Los Angeles Times* (March 3, 1918), quoted in *California News* 33 (May 1918), p. 111.

21. Adolphe Menjou and M. M. Musselman, *It Took Nine Tailors* (New York: McGraw-Hill, 1948), p. 115.

22. Oakland (Calif.) *Enquirer,* quoted in the *Deaf-Mutes' Journal* (February 1920), p. 1.

23. Albert Ballin, "Granville Redmond, Artist," *The Silent Worker* 38 (November 1925), pp. 89–90.

24. All of these films are now available from videotape rental stores and distributors.

25. David Robinson, *Chaplin, His Life and Art* (New York: McGraw-Hill, 1985), is one of the few scholars to identify Redmond as a deaf actor with Chaplin's company, yet he overlooks Redmond's appearance in *City Lights.*

26. In the film *The Pilgrim* (1923), Chaplin pantomimes the biblical story of David and Goliath. Some observers attributed his skill to Redmond's influence, but neither Chaplin nor Redmond spoke on this topic. See *California News* 38 (May 1923), p. 142.

27. Joseph P. Lash, *Helen and Teacher: The Story of Helen Keller and Anne Sullivan Macy* (New York: Delacorte Press, 1980), pp. 470–86. The photograph with Chaplin appears between pages 370 and 371.

28. Mordaunt Hall, "The Screen Column," *New York Times* (September 27, 1926), 27:3.

29. Redmond's biographer, Mildred Albronda, informs me that there is a renewed interest in his paintings, some of which now command prices in excess of $20,000. Personal communication, July 20, 1986.

30. John E. Penn, "A Deaf Movie Star," *The Silent Worker* 39 March 1927), p. 165.

31. Happy Hands Senior Citizen Oral History Interviews, Videotaped Interviews, July 1981, Gallaudet University Archives, Washington, D.C.

32. "David Marvel—Deaf Dancer," *The Silent Worker* 34 (April 1923), pp. 268–69.

33. Albert Ballin, "A New York Deaf Artist at Hollywood," *The Silent Worker* 38 (October 1925), pp. 27–29; Ballin, "The Life of a Lousy Extra," *The Silent Worker* 40 (June 1928), pp. 388–89.

34. Albert Ballin, *The Deaf Mute Howls* (1930), reprinted in *The Deaf Spectrum,* vol. 5 (Beaverton, Oreg.: Deaf Spectrum Inc., 1974) .

35. Contemporary publications in the deaf community, such as *The Silent Worker,* the *Deaf-Mutes' Journal,* and *California News,* described these artists, but when I interviewed deaf senior citizens who were young adults during the silent era, no one remembered seeing a deaf actor in the movies. These same deaf interviewees consistently mentioned Lon Chaney, his deaf parents, and one or more of his films when asked about deaf actors. A general review of student letters and movie schedules at schools for the deaf, as printed in the Little Paper Family during the silent era, yielded only one reference to a deaf actor in a special movie showing. (See *California News* 43 [April 1927], p. 115.) In his news column, "The Itemizer," deaf writer T. H. Estrella referred to a special showing of *You'd Be Surprised* at the Minnesota School in February 1927. In short, deaf actors were not pointed out routinely as potential role models; hence, they were not well known and were quickly forgotten.

36. *Moving Picture World* (March 9, 1916), p. 1700, italics mine.

37. For a summary of Keller's Hollywood experience, see Lash, *Helen and Teacher,* pp. 470–86.

38. Helen Keller, *Midstream: My Later Life* (Garden City, N.Y.: Doubleday, 1930), p. 187.

39. Catherine O. Peare, *The Helen Keller Story* (New York: Thomas Crowell, 1959), pp. 126–28.

40. *New York Times* (August 19, 1919), 10:1; *Variety* (August 22, 1919), p. 76.

41. For the general movie audience, the scene reinforces a popular view of deafness: that making a loud noise behind a deaf person is an accurate test of deafness. For persons familiar with deafness, the scene is intriguing because it is contradictory. A real deaf person would not react as did the valet: because of the vibration, smell (of gunpowder), or some sound, he should have jumped. A disciplined fake, like Silent Smith in *Martyrs of the Alamo,* would not react because this is a traditional test he would expect. In short, many deaf people react to unexpected, nearby loud noises, even though most of them simply cannot discriminate well enough to tell you what the sound is. Unfortunately, we do not know if Redmond apprised the director of this

situation or whether he simply acquiesced in the stereotyped detection of fake deafness.

42. See Hall, "The Screen Column."

43. In the film credits, Robert Benchley is listed as the caption writer.

44. Quoted in *The Silent Worker* 23 (November 1911), p. 55.

45. Elwood Stevenson to Will Hays, March 17, 1931, quoted in *California News* 40 (March 1931), pp. 161–62.

46. "Preservation of the Sign Language," George M. Veditz Film Collection, Edward Miner Gallaudet Memorial Library, Gallaudet University, Washington, D.C.

2

Talking Motion Pictures, 1929–48

Throughout the 1920s, an increasing number of Americans turned to radio as a source of information and entertainment. A few entrepreneurs saw the developing sound technology as an opportunity to provide a new movie product and to earn a profit. In 1925, building on experiments first conducted in the late nineteenth century, Bell Laboratory physicists and engineers perfected the Vitaphone process, which synchronized sound and film. Sam Warner purchased the system. Warner Brothers Studios' competitor William Fox purchased another sound technology in 1926 and perfected Movietone. Both companies invested in the production of new movies with sound and installed their systems in movie houses throughout the country. Seeing the popularity of the new talking motion pictures, the other movie studios followed suit.

Despite, or maybe because of, the hard times Americans encountered during the Great Depression, the movie industry prospered.[1] In 1929, Hollywood produced 335 films, half of them talkies that could not be heard in the more than 10,000 theaters not yet wired for sound; by the end of 1930, studios were no longer making silent films.[2] Responding enthusiastically to the new talking motion pictures, movie audiences increased their attendance; in 1930, moviegoers in the average household saw three movies each week.[3]

In 1927, a *Silent Worker* columnist wondered "how the 'talking movies' are going to affect the deaf. Those who have heard them pronounce the innovation wonderful. So far any comment from a deaf spectator seems to be lacking. It is probable that there will be a curtailment in the acting to give more play to the speech. This would surely detract from the interest of the deaf patron. In cases, if it sent him back to more sensible reading matter, it might not be an unmixed blessing."[4] Two years later, it was clear that the new talking motion pictures, although bothered by technical difficulties, would indeed replace the silent films.

Informing their readers that neither President Calvin Coolidge nor Charlie Chaplin liked the new talking films, deaf newspapers and magazines enthusiastically and regularly reprinted articles that complained about both the films and the quality of the sound.[5] But the industry-wide fear that the current group of stars could not accommodate to the voice requirements of the new technology proved unfounded; with a few exceptions, they made the transition without the help of their well-trained colleagues on the legitimate theatrical stage.[6]

The *New York Times* printed letters of complaint from deaf persons who demanded the return of the silent films or at least the inclusion of captions on the talkies. Oral adult deaf groups insisted that members could not be expected to lip-read the talkies, and the speech-reading club of Philadelphia organized a distribution of antitalkie petitions among all hard-of-hearing clubs.[7] The *Times* noted that "rapid readers have always been struck by the length of time a caption is displayed. They could read it a dozen times over while the rest of the house mumbled it over. . . . This is eliminated by the introduction of speech—it may be tinny but it is intelligible. In the end, it may be competition between those who hear with difficulty and those who can hardly read."[8] The paper also reported that a London theater had installed earphones with a switch that regulated the sound "good for anyone unless the eardrum is completely destroyed."[9] And in its account of a meeting of motion picture engineers in the fall of 1930, the *Times* described movie earphones and claimed that "only ten percent" of the population could not enjoy movies due to defective hearing.[10]

Although deaf persons complained to each other, and a few wrote letters to the editors of major newspapers, there was no widespread, organized protest against the talkies. The National Association of the Deaf (NAD) did not have a permanent headquarters or professional staff and its officers did not yet appreciate the value of political lobbying. (It would be another forty years before deaf groups identified themselves with political and civil rights activists and began to advocate their rights to the arts media.) In 1930 most deaf persons simply reconciled themselves to the takeover by the talkies. Although some continued to struggle for access to the performing arts through the use of captions, interpreters, or deaf repertory companies, an editorial in the widely read *Deaf-Mutes' Journal* reflected the unfortunate reality of the situation: "It is not for the deaf to stand in the way of progress. Neither is it expected that any form of entertainment should be adapted to their peculiar and lamentable condition of being deprived of a sense of sound."[11]

Denied equal access to the new movies, the deaf community turned inward. At Gallaudet College in Washington, D. C., which was then the only institution of higher learning for deaf individuals, a 1930 editorial in the campus newspaper, *The Buff and Blue,* suggested that students present more of their own plays, interspersed with the showing of old silent movies.[12] The college thus became a microcosm of deaf communities throughout the nation. Local publications for deaf persons routinely advertised lectures, skits, plays, dances, old silent movies, and an occasional movie in sign language. Some deaf persons purchased silent films, while others discovered that they could borrow them from universities and special collections. Well into the mid-thirties, deaf organizations advertised the silents or used them to attract deaf persons to attendance at benefits or charitable events.[13] But this increasingly became more difficult as films deteriorated and movie projector speed changed.

The same patterns that filmmakers had used to describe deafness and deaf individuals during the era of silent films continued unabated and unchallenged for the first twenty years of talking motion pictures. Ten movies distributed between 1929 and 1948 reinforce and add to the stereotypes previously established in silent movies. In addition to the "dummy" characters and perfect lip-readers, these films introduced perfect speech among and cures for the deaf.

The Dummy Label

Actors continued to speak lines that refer to deaf characters as deaf and dumb or, more pejoratively, as dummies. *The Dummy,* previously seen as a silent film in 1917, was remade as a talking motion picture in 1929, with a fake "deaf" character. The first talking movie to depict a truly deaf character was *Beau Bandit* (RKO, 1930), a western featuring Rod LaRoque as the Hispanic bandit Montero and Mitchell Lewis as his deaf-mute sidekick Colosso. When one of the villains meets Colosso for the first time, he says to Montero, "You mean he can't hear or talk. He's dumb?" Montero replies, "No, I wouldn't call Colosso dumb." The film nevertheless depicts Colosso as a petty thief who survives outside the law. He and Montero are really "good" bandits, who steal from a ruthless banker and give the money to a young ranch owner to pay off his mortgage and marry his sweetheart. In the interim, Colosso traps and ties up a posse, terrorizes the banker, and remains alert to danger through his ability to feel the vibrations of approaching horses.[14] At film's end, Montero recognizes that he and Colosso have done good deeds but laments the fact that they are penniless, at which point Colosso smiles and pulls a gold watch out of his pocket, stolen from the banker.

This stereotyped mute character became a standard fixture in talking motion pictures. In the silents, films had often linked or confused hearing and speech. Now, the talkies made the same linkage by simply dropping speech or sound when deaf characters were depicted. In spite of the fact that the portrayal of deaf speech was possible now with the talkies, filmmakers required their deaf adult characters to speak perfectly or not speak at all. It was as if scriptwriters and directors were afraid that movie audiences would be offended if they heard an imperfect or real hearing-impaired voice. Not able to speak, the dummy character could not utter a sound, not even a grunt. Colosso became the model for the new stereotype and for the next half century, movie audiences became accustomed to the silent deaf person.

Perfect Speakers

The alternative to the dummy was the deaf character who had perfect speech. Two such characters appear in *The Flying Marine* (Columbia, 1929) and *The Man Who Played God* (Warner, 1932), but since each of them actually was a hearing individual who became deaf accidentally, their clear speech is easily explained. In neither film did the scriptwriters see a need to maintain speech skills through articulation lessons. In the earlier film, the deaf character is cured; and in the latter, all of the remediation focuses on the need to acquire lip-reading skills.

The symbol of the profoundly deaf character who speaks without accent and reads lips perfectly was the actress Loretta Young, who appears as a beautifully costumed, rich, deaf woman in two films: *The Story of Alexander Graham Bell* (Twentieth Century–Fox, 1939) and *And Now Tomorrow* (Paramount, 1944). The first film deals with the inventor's early struggles with the telephone and his subsequent court

battle to retain patent rights. Bell is portrayed by Don Ameche; Young
plays his deaf wife, Mabel Hubbard. Even though the Bells' daughter,
Mrs. Gilbert Grosvenor, served as a technical adviser on the film, a
reviewer who was knowledgeable about the limits of lip-reading observed that Young "understands far more general conversation than the
most expert lip reader could understand."[15] That plus her perfect
speech create an idealized deaf character, although the film does try to
convey some of the difficulties of teaching deaf children when it looks
at Bell's early career as a teacher.

Early in the movie, Bell is asked, "Is it true you can teach dumb
people to talk?" Admitting that he has never done so, Bell explains that
since deaf people cannot hear, one must make speech visible to them,
and if this can be accomplished, "there is no reason why they shouldn't
speak as well as any one of us." Scenes follow that depict Bell's work
with a deaf boy, named George Sanders, using an alphabet glove (a
nineteenth-century device whereby teachers spell words by pointing to
specific spots on the student's hand for each letter of the alphabet).
Mabel Hubbard's father is initially interested in this aspect of Bell's
work and recruits him to tutor his daughter; later he is persuaded to
invest in the telephone. Bell eventually succeeds with little George,
who says with difficulty, "fa . . . fa, fa, father." This is the first
hearing-impaired voice heard by movie audiences and sets the pattern
for future films: if the voice is impaired, it is that of a child; deaf adults
are expected to speak without accent or blemish. Since this film provided no further elaboration, it was reasonable for movie audiences to
assume that Bell's pupil grew up to speak as wei. as Mrs. Bell. The
real George Sanders did not. He became a member of the signing deaf
community, attended Gallaudet College, married a deaf woman, and
became a printer.[16]

Released in 1944, *And Now Tomorrow* marked the return of Alan
Ladd from military service.[17] He plays Merek Vance, who establishes
a medical practice in a company town dominated by the family of a
rich deaf woman, Emily Blair, played by Loretta Young, who communicates through speech and lip-reading. Her communication skills
replicate those depicted in her earlier film; however, the film introduces
medical cures for deafness, in this case via experimental serums.

Early filmmakers were fairly circumspect on the topic of medical
treatment for deafness, but they were blatant in their use of speech as
a symbol for a successful cure of a previously deaf-mute character.

Depressed over his deafness, George Arliss is comforted by his young fiancée, Bette Davis, in this scene from *The Man Who Played God* (Warner, 1932). Courtesy of the Wisconsin Center for Film and Theater Research.

Don Ameche as the young Alexander Graham Bell and Loretta Young as his wife, Mabel Hubbard, in *The Story of Alexander Graham Bell* (Twentieth Century–Fox, 1939). Courtesy of the Wisconsin Center for Film and Theater Research.

Even in the absence of a dramatic film-ending cure, speech remains the most common measure of success for the deaf character—which is pleasing to oralists but is extremely offensive to those deaf people who know what is actually involved in speech acquisition and who know the real possibilities for complete success.

The Fake Deaf Person

Fakes are always mute and they are always men. Filmmakers must presume that deafness emasculates a man and renders him harmless, and is therefore a perfect mask behind which he can deceive his enemies. The fakes in talking pictures are no different than the fakes in the silent movies. Except for the addition of sound, the plots are often the same—as in the remake of *The Dummy* (Paramount, 1929). In *Mountain Justice* (Universal, 1930), a western version of the fake, starring the popular cowboy hero Ken Maynard, the hero's father is shot after receiving a warning letter. Maynard pretends to be deaf in order to force people to write notes to him so he can compare the handwriting in the notes with that in the warning letter.[18] He discovers that the warning came from an attractive woman, and he eventually marries her and captures the murderer.

The Unhappy Deaf Person

Deaf characters continue to appear in films as solitary figures, unhappy, suicidal, and pitied or deceived by friends and family. One of the early talkies, *The Flying Marine* (Columbia, 1929), depicts a stunt pilot who loses his hearing in an accident. His girlfriend and brother work to raise funds for an operation and the two fall in love, but because of his deafness, they pity him and do not inform him of their relationship. When the pilot recovers his hearing through a successful operation, he learns of their affair, begins stunt flying again, saves his brother's life, then crashes and dies.

Although the deaf character is relatively happy at film's end, pity reappears in the 1932 version of *The Man Who Played God*, starring George Arliss. Arliss becomes engaged to his admiring protégé, played by a blonde Bette Davis, and after he loses his hearing, they communicate through written notes. Depressed by his hereditary deafness, he postpones the marriage, sending her away while he retreats to his penthouse apartment: "Go Grace, go back to the world of real people. I am not a man. I am just an empty shell." When his butler brings him another note, Arliss says, ". . . no more writing. Just food and water at mealtimes. I am only an animal now." Then, through lip-reading and personal acts of philanthropy, the former pianist regains his faith in God and his will to live. In the interim, Davis has fallen in love with another, younger man but resolves to marry Arliss because he already is burdened with deafness. (Arliss learns of this when he lip-reads her conversation with her suitor.) Magnanimously, Arliss tells Davis to go to her true love.

Susan Hayward, as the younger sister, and Barry Sullivan, as the fiancé, are not so charitable in the film *And Now Tomorrow*. They take advantage of a deaf Loretta Young, who is heir to the family fortune, and it is only after she is cured that she learns of their schemes, breaks off her engagement to Sullivan, and turns to the doctor who supplied the serum that cured her.

As in the silent movies, no deaf character ever had another deaf friend, let alone a deaf husband or lover, in the early decades of the talking motion picture. This would have pleased Alexander Graham Bell, who, although he did not approve of laws that would make marriage illegal between deaf persons or of forced sterilization of deaf persons, did advocate positive eugenics, a popular concept at the turn of the century. As was the case in his own marriage, he believed that deaf persons should marry individuals with normal hearing in an effort to improve the race. In *The Man Who Played God*, the pianist explains that his mother was deaf, and ". . . her father and his father before him, a terrible inheritance."

The Expert Lip-reader

The most powerful public belief about deaf persons is the one that attributes to them almost magical skills to read lips. In spite of the fact that deaf letter writers complained to local newspapers about the exaggerated lip-reading skills of the deaf characters in silent films, and despite protests from profoundly deaf, hard-of-hearing, and oral deaf groups, as well as the superintendents of schools for the deaf, Hollywood remade films like *The Man Who Played God* with sound and no captions. This was the only film that included lip-reading lessons, and its star, in his autobiography, described these scenes, of which he was quite proud. Arliss found a teacher of lip-reading and asked him to act in the film, "which he did with ease and authority. . . . The result was an attractive little scene which bore a stamp of truth."[19] Claiming that he received more correspondence for this film than any of his other work, Arliss remembered that "one of the most satisfactory letters that reached me was from a group of deaf people who told me that they had never thought of attempting lip-reading until they saw this picture, and that now they were all learning rapidly, and that a new life had opened up to them."[20]

Since all residential schools in the United States in 1940 were dominated by oral educators who required lip-reading as a part of the basic curriculum, one is hard put to understand where Arliss's correspondents came from. Even writers for the *Volta Review,* the official professional journal for oral educators, felt that lip-reading in the film was exaggerated.[21] For example, a physician tells the deaf pianist: "I have known many cases in which deaf people have been saved from despair by learning to read lips. They sometimes become so quick they realize what is being said as rapidly as if they heard." With nothing said about the limits of lip-reading, the deaf character works diligently for several months. As his final test, the lip-reading teacher places his fist in front of his mouth, with only parts of his lips visible. Arliss reads him perfectly and explains that he understands "partially from the lips and the muscles of the jaw." Later, the pianist discovers that, using binoculars, he can read the lips of people in the park below his penthouse apartment.

Filmmakers tied lip-reading directly to a deaf character who uses sign language in *Charlie Chan at the Olympics* (Twentieth Century–Fox, 1936). Played by Warner Oland, Chan pursues the thief of a secret radio-aeroguidance device to Berlin, the site of the 1936 Olympic Games, where, coincidentally, Chan's Number One Son is competing for the United States as a swimmer. When Chan finds the stolen device, foreign spies kidnap his son in an effort to force the detective to divulge the device's hiding place. The spies and Chan agree to meet at the Olympic stadium to discuss terms. In the interim, an industrial competitor across the stadium is able to keep tabs on Chan because he has hired a deaf man to read Chan's lips. The deaf man raises the binoculars to his eyes and with his left hand finger spells to an interpreter the conversation between Chan and the spies. Armed with this knowledge, the industrialist shows up at the rendezvous between Chan and the spies and saves both Chan and his son.

Most deaf-mute characters played minor roles in the films of this era. In *Moonrise* (Republic, 1948), the film's star, Dane Clark, is haunted by his father's execution for the crime of murder. Taunted throughout his childhood, Clark becomes the protector of the local deaf-mute, played by Harry Morgan, who is also teased by local bullies.[22] Clark accidentally kills one of the bullies and escapes undetected. When Morgan finds the murder weapon, Clark nearly strangles him in an effort to take it away. Recoiling at his attack on this "helpless cripple," as the film's publicity kits describe the deaf character, Clark repents and voluntarily confesses his crime, thereby improving his chances for an acquittal.

Out of the Past (RKO, 1947) features Robert Mitchum as a gas station owner who, as a former private investigator, is being sought by a former employer-gangster (Kirk Douglas). One of Mitchum's current workers is a "deaf kid" who engages in the following "conversation" with a thug who is looking for Mitchum:

> THUG: Deaf and dumb, eh?
> DEAF KID: Nods yes.
> THUG: Can you read lips?
> DEAF KID: Nods yes.
> THUG: Where is Bailey [Mitchum]?
> DEAF KID: Points out.
> THUG: Coming back today?
> DEAF KID: Nods yes.

The "deaf kid" eventually saves Mitchum's life.

Between 1929 and 1948, when the deaf community was essentially denied access to talking motion pictures, the image of deaf characters worsened in Hollywood. Despite their technical ability to do so, filmmakers refused to provide captioned summaries of the dialogue, which also meant that when characters used sign language, the hearing audience did not know what was being said. Scriptwriters produced idealized deaf characters who spoke perfectly, or else they reinforced the "dummy" stereotype. Then *Johnny Belinda* (Warner Brothers, 1948) opened in New York and Los Angeles to rave reviews. Most deaf viewers liked the film because, even though it was not captioned, it could be understood thanks to the main character, who was deaf and eventually used signs and finger spelling. And despite the fact that this character was mute and dependent, the film expanded the public's view of deafness.

NOTES

(For film documentation, see the Filmography.)

1. For a discussion of the movies and the depression, see Garth Jowett, *Film: The Democratic Art* (Boston: Little, Brown, 1976) , pp. 196–97.

2. Alexander Walker, *The Shattered Silents: How the Talkies Came to Stay* (New York: Morrow, 1979), p. 203.

3. Jowett, *Film*, pp. 196–97.

4. J. W. Howson, "The Argonaut," *The Silent Worker* 39 (April 1927), p. 2.

5. For example, see "The Talkies," *Deaf-Mutes' Journal* (May 2, 1929), p. 2.

6. Film historians have documented this transition. For example, see Kevin Brownlow, *The Parade Gone By* . . . (New York: Ballantine Books, 1968), pp. 566–77; William K. Everson, *American Silent Film* (New York: Oxford University Press, 1978), pp. 334–47; Walker, *Shattered Silents*, pp. 74–89.

7. *New York Times* (April 2, 1929), 13:3.

8. Ibid. (April 3, 1929), 28:6.

9. Ibid. (July 11, 1929), 15:4.

10. Ibid. (October 24, 1930), 21:2.

11. "Talkies," *Deaf-Mutes' Journal* (July 31, 1930), p. 2.

12. Konrad Hokanson, editorial in *The Buff and Blue* (Washington, D.C.: Gallaudet College, April 1930), pp. 269–70.

13. According to the *Deaf-Mutes' Journal* (September 18, 1930, p. 4), "One of the few places in Los Angeles where silent movies are shown is at the Los Angeles Silent Club." These so-called movie nights started as early as 1920 and eventually became the only choice for movie entertainment for many in the deaf community. See typical advertisements for the period in *Deaf-Mutes' Journal* (March 8, 1935), p. 1; (March 15, 1934), p. 1. Silent movies and home movies for deaf community events were advertised in "Films for Rent," *Deaf-Mutes' Journal* (October 13, 1934), p. 4.

14. This is an early example of the public perception that the loss of one sense enhances the other senses. Research findings consistently demonstrate that deaf persons are no better able to detect vibrations than persons who

hear. See "Tactual Perception," *Gallaudet Encyclopedia of Deaf People and Deafness* (New York: McGraw-Hill, 1986), vol. 2, p. 272. A most recent example of this myth appeared on the television program "Magnum, P.I.: One Picture Is Worth" (CBS, October 8, 1986), wherein a deaf character correctly predicts that an automobile tail pipe is about to drop off the hero's car.

15. Harriet Montague, "We Get into the Movies," *Volta Review* (June 1939), p. 332. Since this article appears in the national journal of oral educators, one must presume that this is a realistic assessment.

16. The early scripts for *The Story of Alexander Graham Bell* include a great deal of dialogue about the history of the Bell family's (grandfather and father) professional expertise with articulation and visible speech. The film's producer, Darryl Zanuck, expressed his disappointment with the detailed background on deafness and told the scriptwriters to get the girl and romance into the story early on. See *"Story of Alexander Graham Bell:* Conference Memorandum from Darryl Zanuck, May 12, 1938," Twentieth Century–Fox Script Collection, Theater and Performing Arts Library Archive, University of California, Los Angeles.

17. Marilyn Henry and Ron De Sourdis, *The Films of Alan Ladd* (Secaucus, N.J.: Citadel Press, 1981), pp. 88–91.

18. The device of catching a crook through the comparison of notes written by or to a deaf person first appeared in the silent film serial *Ashton Kirk, Investigator: Menace of the Mute* (Pathes Freres, 1916).

19. George Arliss, *My Ten Years in the Studios* (Boston: Little, Brown, 1940), p. 178.

20. Ibid., p. 190.

21. In her review of this film, Harriet Montague identified the lip-reading teacher as Dr. E. L. La Crosse, associate principal of the Wright Oral School in New York City, and reported that he helped to "tone down some of the lip-reading prowess as originally portrayed." See Montague, "Deafness in Plays and Stories," *Volta Review* 31 (March 1929), pp. 100–101.

22. *"Moonrise:* Synopsis," Final Continuity Script, Archive of Performing Arts, University of Southern California.

3

The "Dummy" Stereotype Changes, 1948–69

After World War II, the deaf community actively railed against the "dummy" image: "It is the word dumb that we despise, detest, and loathe, for there is among the hearing public a wide misconception of the use of the term dumb in reference to the deaf. . . . many hearing persons are prone to confuse the word dumb with the brains or interpret it as meaning 'one who is stupid and unable to think or reason clearly.' Naturally, deaf persons resent the application of such a phrase to them."[1] Hollywood only half-listened.

Johnny Belinda (Warner, 1948) was the first film to allow a hearing audience to experience vicariously the evolution of a deaf character, Belinda McDonald (played by Jane Wyman), from the negatively stereotyped "dummy" to a human being who happened to be deaf. At the beginning of the film, set in rural Nova Scotia, the entire community, including Belinda's aunt (Agnes Moorehead) and father (Charles Bickford) who have difficulty remembering her real name, calls her the "dummy." Then the new village doctor (Lew Ayres) teaches her signs, numbers, and the manual alphabet, and Belinda is able to communicate her innate intelligence and goodness. As her inner beauty emerges, the local village bully (Stephen McNally) is attracted to her and rapes her. Later, Belinda gives birth to Johnny, and the doctor is ostracized by the village, which is convinced that he is the father. When the bully and his new bride (Jan Sterling) try to take the baby from Belinda, convincing the village that a dummy is an unfit mother, she shoots and kills him. At the subsequent murder trial, the wife admits her husband's paternity and Belinda's actions are seen as self-defense. She is free now to marry her benefactor, the doctor.

In prior films, manual forms of communication often were used for secret communication, excluding even the audience through a lack of

captions. But in *Johnny Belinda* the doctor serves as a voice interpreter, through his appropriate responses to Belinda's silent communication, and thereby permits the audience to participate fully in the
story. Resisting the industry's prior penchant for using signs as gimmicks, this film suggests the power of sign language to enhance the
spoken word.[2] It does so through Belinda's recitation of the Lord's
Prayer after her father is killed accidentally by the bully. Belinda
kneels next to the coffin and silently prays in sign while male voices
serve as her chorus and speak the words.

This prayer scene was the centerpiece of the film and Wyman obviously worked hard to make it succeed. The California Association of
the Deaf had sent its own film of the Twenty-third Psalm to the studio
and expressed the hope that its footage would be used in some way.[3]
Instead, in filmed rehearsal, the technical advisers signed the prayer as
Wyman spoke the words. She then took the rehearsal footage home for
study and practice. When audiences saw the signed prayer on film,
they understood that the signs contributed more than the English alone.
A *Variety* film reviewer enthusiastically praised Wyman's performance: "It is a personal success; a socko demonstration that an artist can
shape a mood and sway an audience through projected emotions without a spoken word."[4]

The fact that Wyman never speaks in the film adds to its power.
Director Jean Negulesco did not succumb to the temptation to use the
stereotyped ending of both the original script and the stage version,
wherein at the conclusion of the trial, when she is acquitted, Belinda
finally talks—pronouncing, with difficulty, the name of her restored
infant son; or in another version of the courtroom scene, she screams
"No" when the doctor is accused of being the child's father.[5] The writers and director understood that Belinda did not have to talk in order
to be a complete human being or to provide a happy ending for the
film. Thus, the film was strengthened by not adhering to the old Hollywood tradition and, incidentally, not insulting the deaf community.

The deaf community cannot claim any credit for the changed ending, however. When the film was in production, letters from the deaf
community focused attention on sign language and the desire that the
signs be done well and with grace. But it was Bruce Carruthers, one
of the technical advisers, who suggested that Stella (Jan Sterling),
the wife of the man killed by Belinda, break down under cross-
examination and admit that her husband had fathered the child, imply-

ing justification for the killing. Carruthers added: "Whether you ever have BELINDA speak or not is not for me to say. . . . I don't know which would be worse to the audience: . . . A very attractive deaf girl who cannot speak or the sound of the rattle of a subnormal voice just before the audience leaves the theatre."[6] Wyman expressed concern about the changed ending, but the director incorporated the suggestion from Carruthers into the film.[7]

Although Jerry Wald, the producer, was enthusiastic about the film's potential as a major box office draw, Warner Brothers delayed its release.[8] Upon distribution, none of the posters or advertisements mentioned the words "deaf" or "sign language." Instead, the publicity department promoted the movie as a rape film: "There was temptation in her helpless silence . . . / Lew Ayres as the doctor first to know her shame! / Wherever motion pictures are shown, this story of a young girl's betrayal is the year's most discussed drama!"[9] However, Lil Hahn, in a newly established movie review column for *The Silent Worker,* spoke for the deaf community when she wrote: "Perhaps the impression left with me is much deeper and lasting than . . . to the average moviegoer. . . . For the first time in screen history, the sign language is presented with beauty and grace for what it is—a pictorial symbolic language. . . . [This is] a deeply humanitarian story that brings to the general public for the first time a sympathetic approach to the deaf."[10] Film reviews in *Variety* and the *New York Times* were equally positive, and the movie industry endorsed the view when it recognized Wyman's performance with an Academy Award.[11]

With *Johnny Belinda* as an example of a film that could deal substantively with deafness *and* earn a profit, filmmakers produced nearly a dozen motion pictures in the 1950s that touched on deafness or deaf characters.[12] Except for two musicals, *Sincerely Yours* (Warner, 1955), a retitled version of *The Man Who Played God,* and *For the First Time* (rel. MGM, 1959), each made use of signs or finger spelling by a central deaf character. Two of the films received critical attention for their stars: Sidney Poitier's first film, *No Way Out* (Twentieth Century–Fox, 1950), and James Cagney in Lon Chaney's biography, *Man of a Thousand Faces* (Columbia, 1957). And, for the first time, three films introduced audiences to the education of deaf and deaf-blind children: *Crash of Silence* (aka *Mandy*) (Ealing Studios, 1952), *The Green Scarf* (B&A Productions, 1954), and *The Story of Esther Costello* (Valiant/Columbia, 1955).

In *No Way Out,* Poitier plays a young black doctor who treats two brothers in the jail ward of a large southern city hospital. When one of the men dies, Poitier questions his diagnosis; convinced that he was right, he discusses the case with his supervisor, a liberal white doctor played by Stephen McNally, and they conclude that an autopsy will resolve any doubts. Their conversation is lip-read by a third brother, George (played by Harry Bellaver), who conveys the young black doctor's concern to Ray, the surviving brother (played by Richard Widmark). Widmark refuses to grant permission for an autopsy, preferring to tell the world that the "nigger" doctor murdered his brother. Linda Darnell, who plays the widow of the deceased brother, and George and Ray all use signs and finger spelling to communicate.[13] Their manual communication is clear but unfortunately the film reverts to the technique wherein the audience is excluded from the signed dialogue, once again reinforcing the lip-reading myth.

Widmark warns Poitier about his brother: ". . . George is quite a guy, he's a dummy but he can read lips a block away. And you got big fat lips, you're a pushover for George. . . . He told me everything about the conversation between you and your boss." (Since Bellaver had been seated down the hall and could only see Poitier and his boss in profile, the audience certainly should have been impressed by his skill.) Sensing that Darnell is sympathetic to the black doctor, Widmark, who has escaped from jail, instructs Bellaver to guard her while he goes off to kill Poitier. Reinforcing the dummy image, George reads a comic book and the widow escapes by tricking him into letting her turn up the volume on the radio, attracting the attention of neighbors, who free her. A deaf viewer commented that "the deaf character in this film is not exactly lovable, but we feel it would be a mistake to condemn the picture. . . . The score stands at one to one, as 'Johnny Belinda' was a major contribution to the cause of the deaf."[14]

Throughout the film there are several opportunities for signed communication. However, unlike *Johnny Belinda,* here the audience is kept in the dark by the lack of captions or interpreters. In one scene, for example, as Ray and George are awaiting the results of the autopsy, Ray taps George on the shoulder and, looking at the black doctor, signs: "He's a dumb nigger. He thinks he'll avoid punishment." George responds in sign: "He doesn't want his wife to see him crying." When his brother's widow enters the room, George signs, "Why don't you sit with your nigger friends?"[15] The hearing audience misses all of this, much as deaf audiences are excluded from the spoken dialogue.

Even though it still made use of the dummy character, *Flesh and Fury* (Universal-International, 1952) introduced audiences to a much more complex treatment of deafness.[16] The film's central character is a deaf boxer, Paul "Dummy" Callan (played by Tony Curtis), whose boxing career is pushed too fast in order to satisfy the ambitions and greed of a blonde, named Sonya (played by Jan Sterling), who promises to marry him when he wins the championship. A visiting magazine writer, Ann Hollis (played by Mona Freeman), signs to Callan during an interview and is surprised to learn that he does not speak, read lips, or use sign language. When questioned about her own manual communication skill, the reporter explains that her deceased father, who was an architect, was deaf. Callan gradually gains confidence in her and admits that he understands sign language, which he learned at school, but that he is ashamed to use it because he thinks it marks him as a dummy.

Hollis takes Callan to a school for the deaf, where he sees the improvements in hearing aids and lip-reading that have occurred since his own schooling. Convinced that he can be helped, Callan undergoes an operation that restores his hearing and follows this up with speech lessons. But when he visits Hollis at her home, he becomes confused by the wealth and language of her family and friends and runs away from this new world of sound to resume training for the upcoming championship bout. Unfortunately, his restored hearing results in his loss of timing as a boxer, causing the scheming Sonya to bet against him and to try to hide a telegram from Callan's doctor advising him that he will lose his hearing if he fights again. Afraid and depressed, Callan fights anyway and, as predicted, does poorly against the champion in the early rounds. Then, near the end of the bout, he loses his hearing, his timing returns, and he goes on to win the fight. Afterward, the new champion recognizes that fear can be worse than deafness, and Callan admits his fear of the world of sound to Hollis, when he realizes that she loves him as a person, not as a meal ticket.

Despite the multiple cures, the film is more sensitive to deafness than any prior motion picture, particularly in its depiction of Callan's confusion when his hearing is restored by the operation. Yet it also retains the stereotype of the deaf person as being dependent on one or more hearing persons: in this case Hollis's father, who depended on his hearing wife and daughter; and Callan, who at first depends on the grasping Sonya and then on Hollis as his bridge to a hearing world.

Man of a Thousand Faces, starring James Cagney as the famous silent film star Lon Chaney, provides another substantive view of deafness. In addition to his rebuttals to disparaging remarks about dummies, freaks, and the deaf and dumb, the film attributes Chaney's identification with humane freaks, "people who are different," to his experiences as a child of deaf parents.[17] Originally, the script "lacked the emotion of a man whose past triggered his future. . . . he deaf-signed as a kid and other kids naturally made fun of him—and that colored his whole career, his whole personality."[18] When Cagney pointed this out, the studio hired Ivan Goff and Ben Roberts to rewrite the story.

In the film, which is the first to deal substantively with the issue of deafness and heredity, Chaney does not tell his wife, Cleva (played by Dorothy Malone), that his parents are deaf; incredibly, he takes her to visit them with no forewarning. Cleva, who is pregnant, realizes that they are deaf when Chaney finger spells the introductions. She becomes upset and runs upstairs, prompting Chaney to ask: "Was it that hard to look at them?" When she responds that she could not stand it, he shouts, "Why, is it because they are different . . . because they can't speak, does that make them freaks?" Now hysterical, Cleva tells Chaney, "Ask them about my baby? Will it be like them? It's in your blood; it could happen again." Then she screams, "I don't want to have it. . . . I don't want to be mother to a dumb thing." Chaney, who has three hearing brothers and a sister, leaves the room and walks out of the house. His deaf mother (played by Celia Lovsky) suspects the nature of the problem, follows him outside, and confronts him, signing, "You didn't tell her your parents were deaf?" When he responds that he expected Cleva to understand, his mother scolds him: "You don't understand your responsibility." Chaney tries to avert his eyes, and in a very typical deaf manner she grabs his chin and forces him to maintain eye contact, then tells him to go to Cleva.

Cleva is later reconciled to having the baby, and when their son, Creighton, is born and she hears him cry for the first time, she believes that he cannot be deaf. But then Chaney and her doctor explain that deafness would not affect the baby's vocal chords, and Cleva is distraught. Several weeks later, Chaney prays in Sign: "Dear God, I never pray for anything. Please let my baby hear and talk. Please God, please." Cleva criticizes his use of signs, asking why she must be excluded from the prayers, and he responds that this is the only way he knows how to pray. Chaney then goes to the baby, claps his hands, and the infant cries.

The Chaneys' troubled marriage eventually ends in divorce and he goes on to pursue a successful movie career. Chaney's second wife, Hazel (played by Jane Greer), and Creighton get along well with Chaney's parents. Creighton learns signs, and as an adult he serves as his father's interpreter during a final deathbed scene after Chaney loses his voice to throat cancer. Even though the use of signs and finger spelling is generally clear throughout the film, this final scene is virtually the only one that is interpreted, as Creighton explains his father's signs to the group assembled around the bed. Despite the substantive discussion of heredity and deafness, the hearing audience is excluded from the recognition that Chaney's deaf mother placed the blame for Cleva's hysteria on him. And although the prayer scene imitates the successful scene from *Johnny Belinda,* it too loses its dramatic effect when the hearing audience is not able to participate but must guess at its content.

In spite of these shortcomings, audience reaction surveys taken at California movie theater previews were consistently favorable on the matter of the sign-language dialogue.[19] *Variety* described the film positively as an "unashamed soap opera tearjerker" and in a backhanded compliment observed, "Cagney gives one of his most notable performances. He has immersed himself so completely in the role that it is difficult to spot any Cagney mannerisms."[20]

Man of a Thousand Faces is also unique because it is the only Hollywood film in more than seventy years to depict a deaf couple. Although their scenes are limited, the fact that the elder Chaneys are happy, wise, and have hearing children stands in stark contrast to the alienation, loneliness, and despair of the deaf characters usually portrayed in the movies. The film, however, still depicts them as mutes; and since their signed communication is never translated for the audience, the mute stereotype overwhelms their positive attributes. It should be noted that deaf people often do not use their voices in public in order to avoid misunderstanding or unwanted attention, but they do use them at home, particularly when they have hearing children, as was the case in the Chaney household. The filmmakers thus lost the opportunity to depict scenes of this nature.

A more traditional theme, including substantial footage of the education of deaf children, occurs in *Crash of Silence* (aka *Mandy*). Much of the story unfolds at the Royal Residential School for the Deaf in Manchester, England, and quite naturally reflects a strong English bias in support of oral education.[21] Other than the continued use of the term "dumb" for persons who do not speak, the film makes no pejorative comments about signs or deaf persons who use sign language. In fact, most reviewers remarked on the film's documentary approach; for example: "The film is a powerful documentary as well as drama—showing in meticulous detail the new and astonishing methods by which speech is for the first time brought to the speechless, and the wonders of lipreading to those who must 'see' the spoken word to 'hear.'"[22]

This movie details the life of a deaf girl, Mandy (played by Mandy Miller), who is isolated from the world after a physician confirms her deafness and informs her parents that, never hearing sound, she "would be dumb, too." Living with her parents in her grandparents' house, Mandy is not given a chance to develop and remains speechless. After she survives a near miss with an automobile, her mother (Phyllis Calvert) takes Mandy to a residential facility for deaf students, where they meet the superintendent (Jack Hawkins) and teachers who provide an opportunity for lip-reading and speech education. However, Mandy does not do well until she moves with her mother into a nearby boardinghouse and attends the school as a day-student. Encouraged by the superintendent's enemies, the father (Terrence Morgan) suspects the mother of an affair and insists that Mandy return home, where she resumes her earlier isolated existence. When she is approached one day by hearing schoolchildren who ask her name and invite her to play with them, Mandy finally speaks and her father, who witnesses this, realizes that the residential school had succeeded after all. He and his wife are reconciled, and Mandy presumably goes off to further her education.

Although Helen Keller was world renowned, audiences had not seen deaf-blind characters on the movie screen since 1919. However, in the English film *The Green Scarf*, set in France, Michael Redgrave stars as an attorney assigned to defend a deaf-blind man named Jacques (played by Kieron Moore) who is accused of murder. Redgrave discovers that even though Jacques refuses to communicate or help in his defense, he is an educated man and has written a successful autobiography, entitled *The Lonely One*. In the course of preparing a defense,

Redgrave calls upon a priest (Leo Glenn), who provides information on Jacques's background, education, and life with his wife-companion (Ann Todd). The plot centers on Jacques's refusal to assist in his own defense because of his belief that his wife committed the murder. Redgrave eventually wins Jacques's freedom and identifies the real murderer through a device that takes advantage of a deaf-blind person's inability to distinguish colors—the green scarf.

The school scenes in this film involve blind children, which is appropriate. Yet even with frame-by-frame analysis, their spelling into the hands is unintelligible, although it approximates the British system of two-handed finger spelling. However, since the setting is France (the French use a one-handed system like American finger spelling), all of the manual communication in these scenes is implausible. More important, in its portrayal of Jacques as a successful author, the film perpetuates the superhero image for the deaf-blind character, established by Helen Keller in *Deliverance*, when in fact a large number of deaf-blind adults are often institutionalized or employed in sheltered workshops. Although filmmakers took Helen Keller as the model, their films consistently emphasized the isolation and vulnerability of deaf-blind characters. In spite of Keller's commitment to speech, Hollywood opted for mute-deaf-blind characters, bound to a companion. The absence of speech neutered the deaf-blind character even further and created a perfect victim.

The Story of Esther Costello also has "an almost documentary quality in showing the patient way a mute can be taught to communicate with the world."[23] In this film, Joan Crawford stars as a rich American visiting her ancestral Irish village. A local priest convinces her to take the dirty, abused, deaf-blind Esther (played by Heather Sears) back to America. After Esther is almost killed by an automobile, Crawford remains at the girl's school and becomes her teacher-companion.[24] When Esther's comparatively brief education is completed, the two are invited to make a speech at a nearby school, which results in an unsolicited contribution. Already personally rich, Crawford (along with Esther) finds purpose in a charitable campaign to help deaf-blind people. In the midst of this activity, Crawford's wayward husband (played by Rosanno Brazzi) returns and proceeds to establish a corrupt campaign that benefits the promoters more than the disabled. Then, in what must stand as the most incredible medical cure in film history, Brazzi rapes the attractive, helpless Esther and the trauma restores her hearing, vision, and speech. Esther puts a halt to the dishonest charity campaign, while Crawford kills her husband and herself.

An almost equally implausible finale occurs in *No Road Back* (rel. RKO, 1956), starring Margaret Rawlings as a nightclub owner named Mrs. Railton. Deaf and blind from a World War II bombing incident, the British club owner speaks but depends on a "hand-tapping" language with her adopted daughter-companion, played by Patricia Dainton. She allows a gang to use her club as a cover for its criminal activities, sending her share of the loot to support her son's medical studies in America. When the son, played by Skip Homeir, returns, he falls in love with and wants to marry his mother's companion, but his plans are interrupted when the gang frames him for murder. His mother comes to his aid when she traps the gang leader in her office and, with the aid of her guide dog, aims a gun at him and forces him to confess. Although she is killed, her son is free to marry the woman he loves.[25]

Three other films from the 1950s deserve some comment. *Sincerely Yours* (Warner/International Artists, 1955), the fourth version of the story of the musician who becomes deaf,[26] served as the movie debut for the popular pianist Liberace. Like his predecessors, Liberace suffers depression, attempts suicide, and is saved by the device of lipreading; and, as in two of the three earlier versions, he is cured.

Although this version downplays the incredible lip-reading feats of *The Man Who Played God,* its benefits continue to be exaggerated with no caveat that relatively few persons become expert lip-readers. Liberace himself wanted to emphasize these scenes, and German binoculars, "used by deaf mutes in Turkey to lipread our diplomats," became central to his salvation.[27] When he completes his lessons, his teacher says: "You are to be congratulated because with lipreading, you can hear again."

As for a real medical cure, the film exercises caution. The doctor diagnoses the cause of Liberace's deafness as otosclerosis (the growth of spongy bone in the inner ear) and advises that although his deafness may be temporary, it eventually will become permanent. He suggests a fenestration operation but cautions that it might not be successful. Liberace's hearing returns briefly and he gives a concert for his fans, only to lose his hearing again. Then, like his predecessors in earlier versions, his faith in God is restored through his own acts of philanthropy and he decides to risk the operation. Cured, he gives a final concert at film's end.

Lew Ayres teaches Jane Wyman the sign for "chicken" in *Johnny Belinda* (Warner, 1948). Courtesy of the Wisconsin Center for Film and Theater Research.

Richard Widmark *(center)* communicates with his deaf brother, played by Harry Bellaver *(left)*, in *No Way Out* (Twentieth Century–Fox, 1950). Courtesy of the Academy of Motion Picture Arts and Sciences.

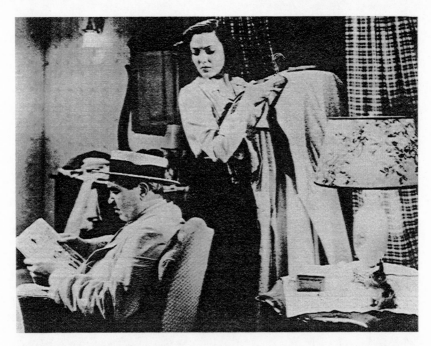

The deaf "dummy" (Bellaver) reads his comic book while sister-in-law Linda Darnell plots her escape in *No Way Out*. Courtesy of the Academy of Motion Picture Arts and Sciences.

A pregnant Cleva Chaney, played by Dorothy Malone *(left)*, first learns that husband Lon Chaney's (played by James Cagney, *third from right*) parents are deaf in *Man of a Thousand Faces* (Universal/International, 1957). Courtesy of the Wisconsin Center for Film and Theater Research.

Joan Crawford *(right)* teaches her deaf-blind ward, played by Heather Sears, to communicate via Braille and finger spelling into the hand, in *The Story of Esther Costello* (Valiant/Columbia, 1955). Courtesy of the Academy of Motion Picture Arts and Sciences.

In one of the few motion pictures that features more than one deaf character, Singer (Alan Arkin, *left*) communicates with his friend, the Greek (Chuck McCann), in *The Heart Is a Lonely Hunter* (Warner, 1968). Courtesy of the Academy of Motion Picture Arts and Sciences.

Singer and his attorney are unable to prevent the Greek from being committed to a state mental hospital, in *The Heart Is a Lonely Hunter.* Courtesy of the Academy of Motion Picture Arts and Sciences.

Anne Bancroft and Patty Duke won Oscars for their performances in Arthur Penn's version of Helen Keller's story, *The Miracle Worker* (United Artists, 1962). Courtesy of the Wisconsin Center for Film and Theater Research.

In another musical released at the end of the decade, *For the First Time* (rel. MGM, 1959), opera singer Tony Costa (played by Mario Lanza), who has a reputation for being difficult because he does not trust anyone, falls in love with a beautiful young deaf woman named Christa (played by Johanna von Koszian). Even though her only flaw appears to be an inability to read lips in the dark, the film depicts Christa as an unhappy victim who refuses to marry Tony unless she can hear. The two go on a European tour, he to sing and she to visit ear specialists. Christa convinces a Salzburg specialist that she will have no life without Tony, and the doctor agrees to perform a dangerous experimental operation. A week later, in the hospital, Christa awakens to Tony singing the "Ave Maria."

The third film, *The Proud Rebel* (Formosa, rel. Buena Vista, 1958), includes a character who can hear but acts like a deaf person. Alan Ladd, his real-life son David, and Olivia de Havilland star in this western tale of a former confederate officer who returns from the war to discover that his wife is dead and his son is gone. He finds his son and their dog in an orphanage and learns that the boy is mute. Without benefit of explanation, the youngster uses signs and finger spells; and, most remarkable, especially for Hollywood, the boy has a voice which is not understandable, even to his father. Unlike deaf children, who speak one word in a dramatic film moment, young David uses a speech-impaired voice with his signs and finger spelling throughout the film; and like earlier deaf-mute characters, he finally speaks clearly at the end of the film.

The father, accompanied by his son and their dog, goes in search of a cure and finds a doctor in a small western town who suggests a surgeon in Minnesota who might help. In the meantime, the local sheep-herding rowdies manage to get Ladd thrown in jail.[28] When he cannot pay the fine, an independent ranchwoman (de Havilland) agrees to let him work out the fine on her ranch. Then, to raise money for his son's operation, Ladd sells the only asset he has—his pedigreed champion sheepdog, a decision he makes only after local children taunt David with the term "dummy." The operation is seemingly unsuccessful; but when Ladd goes off to rescue the dog, which has ended up in the hands of villains, David saves his father's life by yelling "Johnny" when he is about to be shot. Father, son, and the dog return to de Havilland's ranch and with difficulty David says, "Talk, I can talk," at the close of the film.

This movie is inconsistent in interpreting David's manual communication: sometimes his father gives an appropriate response, but frequently the audience is excluded. More important is the confusion of deaf and mute characters. The producers of *Proud Rebel* may have opted for a mute character who uses signing in order to capture more audience interest.[29] In any event, this is one more example of Hollywood's confusing two distinct handicaps—hearing impairment and speech impairment.[30]

On a comparative basis, then, the films that came after *Johnny Belinda* are significantly different than those that preceded it because the deaf characters in later films communicate substantively via a manually coded form of English that makes use of finger spelling and signs from American Sign Language. Although these signed dialogues are not really sign language, general audiences, unfamiliar with the linguistic complexities of ASL, assume that they are watching sign language. With this communication option, these later films more easily portray different types of, and especially more complex deaf characters, even though they continue to depict them as mutes and continue to use the labels "deaf and dumb" and "dummy." Characters who use signs in these films receive more attention and development; however, the other stereotyped characters who speak fluently and read lips without miscue continue to appear, although not as frequently as the mute characters. In the next decade there would not be many deaf characters in major American films, and those that do appear are clones from the fifties.

Not Much Progress, 1960–69

The first film of the decade that featured a deaf character was *Pocketful of Miracles* (United Artists, 1961), in which Ellen Corby plays a deaf-mute flower peddler—one of several disabled peddlers that include a dwarf, a blind man, and a double-leg amputee—on Broadway during the depression. They all take orders from Apple Annie (played by Bette Davis), to whom they each must pay for the right to "work" the territory; Annie uses the money to support her daughter's education in Europe. In this adaptation of a Damon Runyon story, the disabled characters help Annie maintain the fiction, for the sake of her daughter, that the gin-swilling but good-hearted peddler boss is a lady of great wealth and social standing. When an imminent visit by Annie's daughter and her fiancé promises to reveal Annie's true station in life, she is saved with the help of Duke (played by Glenn Ford), who depends on Annie's apples for good luck. (At the outset of the film, Duke asks why the apples are lucky and Annie explains that the "little people [leprechauns] like children, beggars, and poets.")

Corby uses sign language throughout the film and has her words interpreted by the other disabled peddlers. Although her character represents a substantial improvement over the petty thief Colosso, the first talking motion picture deaf character thirty years earlier, the fact remains that she is a peddler—the first to appear in a Hollywood film—in spite of the fact that the deaf community had waged active anti-peddler campaigns throughout the forties and fifties. And in case anyone in the audience has missed the negative stereotypes, Ann-Margret (who plays the daughter) tells Apple Annie that she received a gift of a flower, while walking down Broadway, from "a little old flower peddler, a deaf and dumb lady." *Pocketful of Miracles* is also unique because it is the only American talking motion picture *comedy* in which a deaf character appears—filmmakers generally reserve deaf characters for melodrama.

All of the other films of the sixties that depict deafness do so in the traditional manner, and one of the most successful of these is *The Miracle Worker* (United Artists, 1962), which brought the Broadway stage stars Anne Bancroft and Patty Duke to Hollywood.[31] Drawing on material from Helen Keller's autobiography, the playwright and screenwriter William Gibson here focuses all of the dramatic energy on the teacher, Anne Sullivan, and the task of communicating one word, one concept to her deaf-blind charge, Helen Keller, so that education can begin. The confrontation between the strong-willed teacher and the equally strong-willed girl takes place as Sullivan works to make Helen understand that the manual alphabet that is spelled into her hand incessantly is a means of communication, not merely a game. The intervening dinner-table fight is legendary, both on Broadway and in Hollywood.

The manual alphabet is used clearly throughout the film, and, in addition, the racial stereotypes present in the silent film version, *Deliverance,* have been eliminated. However, the symbol of success still remains speech, although this device is not used as blatantly as the 1919 "I-am-not-dumb-now" caption that resulted in tears among the audience. In *The Miracle Worker,* Helen's father (Victor Jory) gives

Sullivan only two weeks, alone, to make some kind of progress with her deaf-blind student. Although she had taught Helen table manners, Sullivan has not achieved a breakthrough with finger spelling before they must return to the main house. When Helen throws a tantrum, Sullivan confronts her and the child splashes water in her teacher's face. Then, in one of Hollywood's most dramatic moments, Sullivan drags Helen to the water pump to refill a pitcher and Helen remembers a word she spoke as a baby—"wa-wa." She finger spells the word "water," which is the breakthrough Sullivan had worked for, and proceeds to run around the yard asking for the names of everything she touches, including her mother and finally her teacher.

Although moviegoers could see more than a dozen films that portrayed deafness or deaf characters during the sixties, few of them introduced anything new.[32] This was equally true for most of the foreign films that were shown in the United States during this period. In three of these, deaf-mute women die or are killed, usually after being raped: from Great Britain, *The Curse of the Werewolf* (Hammer, 1960); from France, *The Murder Clinic* (Leone-Orphee, 1969); and from Greece, *The Fear* (Trans-Lux, 1967). *The Curse of the Werewolf,* for example, portrays a deaf servant girl who is raped by a beggar and then dies giving birth to an infant werewolf son. In an adaptation of a story by Turgenev, the Russian film *Mumu* (Mosfilm, 1961), depicts a lonely deaf-mute fieldhand who seeks love but is ordered to kill his beloved dog (named Mumu because that is the only sound he can articulate). Winner of the Moscow Film Festival Award for short subjects, another Russian film, *Ballad of Love* (Riga Films, 1966), features a deaf dancer who falls in love with a hearing musician.

Japanese films appeared to differ from these other stereotyped foreign entries, especially *Happiness of Us Alone* (Tokyo Eiga, 1962) and *Our Silent Love* (Tokyo Eiga, 1969). Noting that the "dialogue is easily understood due to the use of English subtitles" in spite of the actors' use of Japanese sign language, a *Silent Worker* movie commentator observed that the story of *Happiness of Us Alone* ". . . is a sad one depicting conditions unknown to the deaf of the U.S., [but] it has its happy moments and even happier ending. . . ."[33] An important Japanese actress, Hideko Takamine, sometimes referred to as the Mary Pickford of Japan, stars as the deaf wife and mother. She is married to a deaf man; the two earn a living by shining shoes. Their first child, who crawls outside into the snow, dies when the deaf couple cannot hear his cries. Another child is born and in later years, after a suicide attempt (she is saved by her husband), the woman realizes that she is a successful wife and mother when that second child graduates from school with honors.[34] In *Our Silent Love,* a young Japanese man cannot obtain a good job because his parents are deaf. A factory owner, who sees the young man as a prospective match for his own deaf daughter, offers him a job. His plan backfires, however, when the deaf daughter and her deaf lover are nearly driven to suicide by the father's concern about hereditary deafness. The young man encourages the deaf couple to marry in spite of the family's objection.

Like most subtitled foreign films, these Japanese movies did not have a large American audience. In their depiction of the deprivation and despair of deaf characters, they are like so many others; however, their solutions to the conditions they depict are different. For example, the perspective that deaf couples represent a source of strength in overcoming the adversity suffered by deaf individuals is unique. Both films portray the discrimination that deaf persons experience in Japanese society,[35] yet the filmmakers, unlike their American counterparts, resolve the difficulty by allowing deaf characters to have deaf lovers and deaf spouses, who together face an otherwise hostile society.

Zenzo Matsuyama served as the scriptwriter and director for both films. A product of the Kinoshita school of Japanese cinema, Matsuyama, like his master, Keisuke Kinoshita, produced films that emphasize themes of innocence and purity.[36] Deaf characters certainly provided Matsuyama an opportunity to pursue these themes, and the result was unique for American audiences.[37] Although a backhanded compliment, Matsuyama makes the point that even deaf people can succeed if they adhere to the traditional values of loyalty, family, and hard work.

Two films released near the end of the decade, *Psych-Out* (Dick Clark Enterprises, 1968) and *The Heart Is a Lonely Hunter* (Warner, 1968), reflect the lack of deaf couples in American cinema. The first, an exploitative film of the hippie and drug culture of San Francisco, includes an excellent cast: Susan Strasberg as Jenny, a deaf runaway; Jack Nicholson as Stoney, a rock musician; Dean Stockwell as Dave, a drug addict; and Bruce Dern as Jenny's brother. Jenny is the now-familiar stereotypical attractive deaf female who speaks clearly, reads lips with few miscues, and is courted and saved by hearing males. In an early scene, she is nearly hit by a car and is accused by its driver of being a drug addict; when the man and his wife learn that Jenny is deaf, the wife says: "Oh, poor little thing, she can't hear." Jenny meets a band of rock musicians, who befriend her and assist in the search for her brother; the band's leader, Stoney, is searching for his own identity, whether in music or in the easy drug culture that surrounds him. Thinking he might have information about her brother, Stoney leads Jenny to Dave, who gratuitously remarks, "She's lovely man, y'know I like sound but sometimes I prefer silence." Stoney is not sure if he should pursue a relationship with Jenny, who obviously is repelled by the drug-related experiences she encounters in the search for her brother. Then, after Dave slips her a drugged drink, which causes her to hallucinate and stagger onto a busy freeway, to be saved from onrushing cars by a repentant Dave (who is killed), Stoney comforts her and they both presumably opt for the straight life.

Another stereotype, the "dummy," or deaf-mute character, appears in the 1968 film *The Heart Is a Lonely Hunter,* based on a prize-winning novel by Carson McCullers. The deaf character, John Singer (played by Alan Arkin), serves as the symbol of an existential human environment where individuals lead lives of alienation and loneliness, uncommunicative and voiceless; of all the people in the story, it is the deaf man who listens. Unlike any other American film before it, this one allows a major deaf character to have a deaf friend. The story revolves around Singer, who moves to a new town near a mental hospital where his lifelong friend, a Greek named Antonapoulos (played by Chuck McCann), is a patient. Singer meets the young daughter of his new landlord, a black doctor, and a drunk, each of whom discovers that it is possible to talk to the lip-reading deaf-mute, who is himself a sympathetic listener. Yet Singer can only communicate freely, in sign language, with Antonapoulos, and when the Greek dies, Singer despairs and kills himself.

Alan Arkin received an Academy Award nomination for his portrayal of Singer, and a *New York Times* film reviewer described his performance as "extraordinary, deep and sound"; "his use of his hands seems quite normal and personal, and when he walks in the night, talking, with his hands to himself, it seems a perfect dramatic expression of what thinking is." In fact, this film review was a perfect example of the abysmal lack of understanding of deafness and the power and beauty of sign language. And it was particularly insulting since the year before, in 1967, deaf actors of the newly created National

Theatre of the Deaf had demonstrated their skills on national television.

The production company and the interracial cast were very proud of the fact that the movie had been shot on location, in Selma, Alabama, the site of comparatively recent civil rights protests. However, the rights of deaf persons apparently were not considered; indeed, the use of hearing actors to portray deaf characters is analogous to the old practice of white actors in blackface portraying black characters. Unlike the narrative form of McCullers's novel, here the audience can see the communication between Singer and Antonapoulos. Yet the film perpetuates the myth that deaf people are mute. Also, the signing is awkward at best, and words are often misspelled or signs are incorrectly executed. These weaknesses are especially clear in the early scenes, which contrast the two characters: Antonapoulos, an illiterate, obese man dominated by gluttonous urges; and Singer, an impeccable dresser, attired conservatively in coat, tie, and hat, who lip-reads perfectly and writes notes in correct English.

Even before the opening credits we see Antonapoulos break a bakery store window in order to devour the display of cookies and a wedding cake. Unable to hear the ringing of the burglar alarm system, the deaf Greek happily stuffs himself as the police arrive to take him away to the local jail. After securing his release, Singer scolds his friend that he is a "bad boy," to which the Greek replies, "I'm a good boy," rejoined by Singer's "bad." As they pass the boarded-up bakery window, the Greek pulls out of his pocket the plastic bride and groom from the stolen wedding cake, and the two laugh uproariously. The next scene, still part of a lengthy prologue, shows Singer at his job as an engraver at a jewelry store. Antonapoulos appears with a note pinned to his shirt, which Singer reads and learns that the Greek's cousin has decided to commit him to a mental hospital; the note asks Singer to get his friend packed and ready for the trip. Singer's lawyer is unable to prevent Antonapoulos's hospital commitment but promises to help Singer find another jewelry store job in a town near the mental institution. The title and credits appear as Singer is moving to the new town.

These early scenes establish the tone of the rest of the film in terms of deafness: the deaf men are silent and their signed and finger-spelled dialogue is not interpreted for the audience. Like Belinda McDonald's noiseless childbirth in *Johnny Belinda* two decades earlier, the laughter these two men share is silent, depicted in pantomime. And despite their differences in intelligence and temperament, both characters are referred to as "dummies": when Singer tries to convince the Greek's cousin not to commit him, the cousin explains that he no longer will be responsible for "the dummy"; when Singer himself seeks lodging in the new town, his prospective landlord's daughter, explaining to her younger brother that "there is a deaf-mute person looking at the room for rent," answers his question, "A what?" with "a dummy"; and when a drunk befriended by Singer leaves town, he says, "I'll miss you—I could talk to you. You listened, you old dummy, you really listened."

The only other person with whom Singer can communicate in sign language is a black patient of the town's black doctor. Singer is asked to help the doctor communicate with the man, who is played by Horace Oats, Jr., not an actor but a real deaf person. In the scenes where Singer serves as the patient's interpreter, writing notes and lip-reading the doctor, the disparity in the communication skills of the real deaf man and the actor, Arkin, is readily apparent to anyone conversant with the language of signs.

While each of the major characters must deal with personal loneliness and alienation, and each talks to Singer, he is not allowed to develop these relationships or teach anyone how to finger spell or sign. No one at the hospital bothers to tell him that the Greek has died, and when he learns of the death on a visit, Singer kills himself. At film's end, the landlord's daughter (Sondra Locke) arranges flowers at his grave and says: "Mr. Singer, can you hear me, I want you to know, I love you." Singer, the film's hero, sensitive toward and caring of the people around him, in the end had won their trust and love.

Nearly a decade later after the film was released, the director, Robert E. Miller, appeared as a guest lecturer at a screenwriting workshop at the American Film Institute in Los Angeles. Much of the discussion centered on *The Heart Is a Lonely Hunter;* two of the workshop participants included deaf actors Gregg Brooks and Kevin Van Wieringer. When Miller commented that the character of Antonapoulos was difficult because of his inability to communicate, the deaf actors joined the discussion and pointed out that even deaf people with limited English skills can communicate meaningfully. To demonstrate their point, they played the restaurant scene wherein Singer takes the Greek on a day's outing and can only get him to return to the mental hospital by bribing

him with a box of candy. Their ASL dialogue was voiced for Miller
and the other workshop participants:

SINGER: Enjoy your food?
GREEK: Love eat food. Love food, love.
SINGER: Me know you love food, but you fat.
GREEK: Don't care. Me healthy. Me don't care.
SINGER: Me think you body feel big.
GREEK: Me ok, me ok.
SINGER: [looking at watch] Time go now. Time gone finish. Officer mad.
    Officer mad.
GREEK: Don't care. Mad me, don't care.
SINGER: Anyway, follow help. Must go back. Tell officer. [pause] Me
    go. You wait.

The deaf actors insisted that they were not being critical but wanted
the film director to understand that a deaf character like Antonapoulos
might not communicate in Standard English but that with the help of
his deaf friend he could communicate meaningfully. Miller accepted
the exchange of information and observed that their dialogue had been
"fascinating and actually it's more dramatic."[38]

In spite of Miller's receptivity to the deaf actors' critique, the exchange demonstrates that filmmakers, among others, do not understand much about deafness or deaf persons. Uninformed about the expressive power of sign language, scriptwriters lose the opportunity to
develop the character of deaf persons and directors accept performances from hearing actors such as Arkin and McCann when in fact
they do not have or portray well the skills appropriate to the deaf characters. In truth, American filmmakers have not made much progress in
the depiction of deafness since the first sympathetic treatment of a deaf
character in *Johnny Belinda*. In the succeeding two decades, the deaf
community, which now had the National Theatre of the Deaf as a
model, began to complain of these long-standing practices by the motion picture industry.

NOTES

(For film documentation, see the Filmography.)

1. William Marra, "Not 'Dumb,'" *The Frat* (November 1948), p. 5.
2. No film has ever explained that American Sign Language is a language

and not simply a manual representation of English. In fact, the academic community in 1948 had not yet recognized or articulated such a linguistic point of view. *Johnny Belinda* comes as close as any film until the appearance of *Children of a Lesser God* in 1986.

3. *"Johnny Belinda:* Leo Jacobs, Publicity Chairman, California Association of the Deaf, to Jerry Wald, October 14, 1947," Correspondence Folder of Producer Jerry Wald, Warner Brothers Collection, Archive of Performing Arts, University of Southern California (hereafter, USC Archives).

4. *Variety* (September 15, 1948), p. 15.

5. *"Johnny Belinda:* Scripts," United Artists Collection, box 208, folders 1–8, Wisconsin State Historical Society, Wisconsin Center for Film and Theater Research (hereafter, Wisc. Archives). However, the 1958 teleplay version, which stars Julie Harris, returns to this theme, which incorporates speech in the climax when Belinda speaks the name of her infant son. See "Hallmark Hall of Fame: Johnny Belinda" (October 13, 1958), Museum of Broadcasting, T85:0053, 54; see also the Filmography.

6. *"Johnny Belinda:* Bruce Carruthers to Jean Negulesco, Undated Memorandum," Research Record, Warner Brothers Collection, USC Archives.

7. "Frank Mattison to T. C. Wright, November 4, 1947," Interoffice Communication, ibid. The writers alleged that both Wyman and Ayres were concerned since the climactic scene would shift from them to the character played by Jan Sterling.

8. Wald was frustrated by the studio's apparent reluctance to provide full support for the film. He reminded Warner Brothers that he had been successful in the past and that he deserved credit for his ability to recognize a good story. For a general discussion of Jack Warner's reluctance to release the film, see Joe Morella and Edward Epstein, *Jane Wyman, a Biography* (New York: Delacorte Press, 1985), pp. 132–34.

9. *"Johnny Belinda:* Pressbook," C-119, Motion Picture, Broadcasting, and Recorded Sound Division, Library of Congress (hereafter, LC).

10. Lil Hahn, "Movie Guide," *The Silent Worker* (November 1948), pp. 24–25.

11. *New York Times* (October 2, 1948), 11:2; *Variety* (September 15, 1948), p. 15.

12. See the Filmography. Television easily matched this outpouring with at least twenty episodes involving deaf characters on various programs between 1950 and 1959.

13. Valentine Becker, California State Rehabilitation Officer for the Deaf, served as technical adviser and sign-language teacher. See *"No Way Out:* Memorandum from Harry Brand, Director of Publicity, Twentieth Century–Fox," Clipping File, Academy of Motion Picture Arts and Sciences (hereafter, AMPAS) .

14. "Just Conversation," *The Silent Worker* (September 1950), p. 31.

15. The printed script confirms this translation of the film dialogue. See *"No Way Out:* Dialogue and Continuity," Twentieth Century–Fox Collection, 2420.11, reel 9, p. 7, USC Archives.

16. *"Hear No Evil,* aka *Flesh and Fury:* Revised Final Screenplay," Leonard Goldstein Collection, AMPAS.

17. For a discussion of Chaney's early life, see Robert G. Anderson, *Faces, Forms, Films: The Artistry of Lon Chaney* (Cransbury, N.J: A.S. Barnes, 1971), pp. 15–20.

18. Ben Roberts, quoted in Patrick McGilligan, *Cagney, the Actor as Auteur* (San Diego, Calif.: A. S. Barnes, 1975), pp. 230–33.

19. *"Man of a Thousand Faces:* Reports on Preview Comments," Universal Collection, 12280, box 412, USC Archives.

20. *Variety* (July 17, 1957), p. 6.

21. See the *Manchester Guardian Weekly* (August 7, 1952) in *"Mandy,* aka *Crash of Silence:* Clipping File," AMPAS.

22. *Cue* (February 28, 1953), pp. 26–27. For a discussion of *Mandy*'s place in the history of Ealing Studios, see Pam Cook, *"Mandy:* Daughter of Transition," in *All Our Yesterdays: 90 Years of British Cinema,* ed. Charles Barr (London: British Film Institute, 1986), pp. 355–61.

23. *Variety* (August 21, 1957), p. 6.

24. Although Sears's finger spelling tends to mistakes more often than not, Crawford's demonstrations of the manual alphabet, braille reading, and lip-reading via touch are clear and accurate. In later years, Crawford observed that "this was my last really top picture, and frankly . . . I deserved two [Oscars]." Quoted in Roy N. Newquist, *Conversations with Joan Crawford* (Secaucus, N.J.: Citadel Press, 1980), p. 104.

25. *"No Road Back:* Publicity Release," Copyright Registration Material, PA 255–100, LC.

26. These stories were credible due to the true-life account of the great composer Beethoven (1770–1827), who became profoundly deaf. When his friends remind him of Beethoven's courage, the deaf character in *Sincerely Yours* reminds them that Beethoven was a composer, not a pianist—hence, hearing was not essential to Beethoven. For other examples of deafened musicians, see "Musicians," *Gallaudet Encyclopedia of Deaf People and Deafness* (New York: McGraw-Hill, 1986), vol. 2, pp. 216–17.

27. *"Sincerely Yours:* Irving Wallace, Report on Story Conference with Liberace, January 10, 1955," Warner Brothers Collection, box 2067, USC Archives.

28. The filmmakers confounded the stereotyped image of disabled persons by depicting the villainous father of the rowdy sheepherders as a one-armed amputee (played by Dean Jagger) .

29. Another variant on the use of signs was with Indians. In *The Big Sky* (Winchester, rel. RKO, 1952), Elizabeth Threatt plays a Blackfoot Indian princess who speaks no English but uses the signs of the Plains Indian tribes.

30. Another example of exaggerated lip-reading occurs in an FBI docudrama, *Walk East on Beacon* (RD-DR Pictures, rel. Columbia, 1952), when a film of the conversation between foreign spies is taken to the "Plummer School of Lipreading," where a student translates the message that leads to the capture of the spies. Although the film makes no reference to deafness, there also is no explanation of why the students were taking a lip-reading course.

31. *The Miracle Worker* first appeared as a teleplay with Teresa Wright and Patty McCormack in the leading roles. See "Playhouse 90: The Miracle Worker" (February 7, 1957), T77:0111, 112, Museum of Broadcasting (New York).

32. A deaf maid appears in Alfred Hitchcock's *Marnie* (Universal, 1964), a fake deaf husband tries to kill Marcello Mastroianni in *Casanova, '70* (Embassy, 1965), and a deaf killer is featured in a low-budget thriller with no spoken dialogue in *Weekend of Fear* (J-D Productions, 1966).

33. This particular comment appeared in *The Silent Worker* (March 1962) and was picked up by the film company and included in its press releases. See "*Happiness of Us Alone:* Clipping File," AMPAS.

34. American reviewers agreed that virtue resulted in happiness, even for a deaf family: "Their honest perseverance pays off as this unusual family emerges as a loving, self-respecting unit" (*New York Times* [April 10, 1963], 31:5); ". . . generosity and need could make a happy marriage, even if husband and wife were deaf and dumb" (Donald Richie, *The Japanese Movie: An Illustrated History* [Tokyo: Kodansha International, 1966], p. 163) .

35. Several writers on Japanese cinema have referred to widespread discrimination in Japanese society and the tendency to "shun handicapped persons as if the affliction is communicable." See, for example, Joan Mellon, *The Waves at Genji's Door: Japan through Its Cinema* (New York: Pantheon Books, 1976), p. 347.

36. For a discussion of the Kinoshita school of cinema, see Audie Bock, *Japanese Film Directors* (Tokyo and New York: Kodansha International, 1978), pp. 248–50.

37. *Children of Silence* (Hanabusa Educational Films, undated), a Japanese documentary film available at Gallaudet College, features the same themes. Directed by Taisuko Nishio, the first half of the film depicts the story of Kenji, a deaf boy who has not learned the difference between right and wrong. When he is nearly hit by a truck he cannot hear approaching, his mother takes him to a school for the deaf, which provides a documentary explanation of Japanese pedagogy, featuring sign language, lip-reading,

speech, and auditory training. The second half of the film depicts the story of Michiko, a young deaf woman who is a graduate of the same school and who returns to seek advice from her teacher. Michiko wants to marry another deaf-mute, Ikeda, who is a leader of the "Deaf and Dumb Society." The teacher and the school principal support her and help her prepare for the wedding. At film's end, Michiko appears at the school in her wedding dress, where she is greeted and congratulated by the entire student body. This film received a prize from the Japanese ministry of welfare, which would imply at least an indirect endorsement of its opening prologue: "all children have the right . . . to lead a full and proper life."

38. Robert E. Miller, Transcript: American Film Institute Screenwriting Workshop, March 22, 1977 (Beverly Hills, Calif.: Center for Advanced Film Studies, 1977), pp. 2, 13–19.

4

Deaf Actors Appear,
1970–86

Very few of the films made during the seventies depict deafness, and in nearly all of them deaf characters are used only symbolically. Opening airport scenes from *Harry in Your Pocket* (United Artists, 1973) feature a deaf victim of a pickpocket; and a mute Indian, Chief Cut-Tongue, uses signs to communicate with Richard Boone in the western *Against a Crooked Sky* (Doty-Dayton, 1975). The only substantial deaf character prior to 1979 appeared when Anthony Quinn starred as a deaf-mute gunfighter in the Italian-made western *Deaf Smith and Johnny Ears* (rel. MGM, 1973).[1] Besides these comparatively low-budget films, Hollywood produced three major motion pictures in the mid-seventies that received a great deal of publicity; and each of them features deafness symbolically: *Nashville* (Paramount, 1975), *Tommy* (Columbia, 1975), and *Looking for Mr. Goodbar* (Paramount, 1977).[2]

In *Nashville,* director-producer Robert Altman expresses his view of American culture via a cynical examination of a host of superficial individuals who work in or wish to take advantage of the country and western music industry. By and large the characters are superficial and incapable of real communication. One of them, a white gospel singer (played by Lily Tomlin) works with a black choral group. Tomlin is married and the mother of two deaf children (played by real deaf children, James Don Calvert and Donna Denton); that she does not communicate her true feelings to her husband is exemplified by the fact that only she communicates with the children through a form of total communication (signs, finger spelling, and speech). Tomlin's scenes reflect the pressures that sometimes exist in a family with deaf children. Usually, it is the mother who accepts responsibility for communication with the child; and these marriages are often unstable (statistically, the incidence of divorce for families with disabled children is higher than that for the general population).

An even more explicit use of a deaf-blind character as the ultimate victim is contained in Ken Russell's *Tommy*. A *Wall Street Journal* film reviewer observed that "if we wanted to put artifacts into a time capsule to represent and summarize '60s pop culture for future generations . . . we could simply use [*Tommy*].³ The film, a rock opera performed to the music of Peter Townshend and The Who, depicts the life of Tommy (played by The Who's lead singer, Roger Daltrey), who became deaf, dumb, and blind after watching his father die. When his mother (played by Ann-Margret) is not taking Tommy in search of miracle cures from such saviors as the Acid Queen (played by Tina Turner), she leaves him at home with "caring uncles and cousins" who abuse him. Tommy rises above this misery and becomes a world-class pinball machine player. With his attendant fame comes wealth, and eventually his hearing, speech, and sight return. Tommy then rejects his wealth to become a new messiah for his cult followers, who wear dark glasses and have corks in their ears and mouths. He delivers a voiceless sermon in a meaningless parody of signs and gestures to a group of wheelchair-bound cerebral-palsied followers who replicate his sign parody. At film's end, the followers rebel, kill his mother, and tear down the temple. Tommy walks into the ocean and emerges on a mountaintop as his own image is silhouetted by a rising sun. *Tommy*, of course, has no significance for deafness but it represents a low point in the depiction and parody of disability in the guise of the filmmaker's art.

Although very different in tone and approach, *Looking for Mr. Goodbar* also appealed to a youth-oriented market in its portrayal of Theresa (played by Diane Keaton), who struggles with the values of her Catholic upbringing and her father-dominated family. By day she works as a teacher of deaf children, and in these scenes the film features all aspects of total communication: hearing amplification, lipreading, speech, signs, and finger spelling. (The children in her classroom are obviously deaf children who speak with hearing-impaired voices, and the purpose of these scenes is made explicit early in the film when Theresa's college professor tells the class, "If you can teach a deaf child, you have touched God."⁴) However, because of her own congenital curvature of the spine and the failed marriages of her parents and her sister, Theresa rejects marriage for herself and opts for the singles life, cruising the bars of Manhattan at night. Her life becomes increasingly tainted by the dangerous use of drugs and sexual partners, and at film's end she is raped and murdered.

Voices (MGM, 1979) stands out from the other films of this decade in that it is a love story involving a deaf woman, Rosemarie (played by Amy Irving), and a hearing man, Drew (played by Michael Ont-kean). Rosemarie is a physical education teacher of deaf children and aspires to be a professional dancer; Drew is a truck driver for his family's cleaning business and aspires to be a successful musician-singer. In their depiction the writers and cast provided generally accurate information and insights about deafness and deaf people. The filmmakers clearly benefited from the example of television (see chapter 5), as they too include scenes that demonstrate various facets of a deaf person's daily life, from the technical gadgetry of doorbell and telephone lights to telecommunication devices.

The film employed two deaf men: Richard Kendall, an actor from the National Theatre of the Deaf, appeared briefly as Rosemarie's fiancé, Scott; and Martin Sternberg, a faculty member at New York University, as the film's technical adviser. And Amy Irving's sister, who is a trained teacher of the deaf, at the time of the filming was employed at the highly reputable Maryland School for the Deaf. In short, the filmmakers and cast had access to a great deal of knowledge about many aspects of deafness. The treatment of two subjects in particular reflects insight and careful research: the topic of the mother's objection to a "mixed" courtship and possible marriage between hearing and deaf persons; and Drew's effort to get Rosemarie to use her voice.

Rosemarie's deaf boyfriend, Scott, is introduced briefly and early in the film; although their signed communication is neither interpreted nor captioned, the audience is made aware of their relationship. Drew, who is attracted to Rosemarie, badgers her for a date, even a simple cup of coffee together. She is also attracted to him and finally relents, inviting him to her house. Prior to his visit, Drew obtains a sign-language book from the library and practices a few phrases. Shortly after he arrives at Rosemarie's house, her mother (Viveca Lindfors) comes home and carries on extended oral conversation with Drew, periodically explaining to Rosemarie what is being said. When Rosemarie learns that her mother has mentioned Scott, probably to discourage Drew from being interested in her, she becomes upset and tells Drew they must leave. They go to a café, but the evening is a disaster. On the way home,

Drew asks Rosemarie, who is a good lip-reader, just how much she understands when he talks; she gestures "only half." Drew is visibly dejected, but when Rosemarie insists that their relationship will not work, he wants to try again. After he leaves, she enters the house and the audience hears her cry out in a deaf wail.

Drew is persistent. He practices finger spelling and goes to Rosemarie's school and watches her dance. In the park one evening they carry on a meaningful sign-and-gesture conversation. As they get to know each other, Drew says that he wants to hear her voice and asks her to talk to him. Reluctantly, Rosemarie says his name and comments in her impaired voice, "I don't sound good." He responds that he cares for her and it does not matter what she sounds like. The film makes it clear that many deaf persons prefer not to use their voices in public or with strangers to avoid misunderstandings or embarrassment.

Caught in a rainstorm, Rosemarie and Drew seek shelter at his house. He has a warm, close-knit family who easily accepts Rosemarie and her deafness; in fact, hearing her speak, his younger brother says, "Your voice isn't bad; sounds foreign." Returning home the next morning, Rosemarie is lectured by her mother on the dangers of a "mixed" relationship with a man who can hear. Lindfors struggles to convey her heartfelt message in awkward signs and finger spelling, like many parents of deaf children who have never learned to communicate easily with their offspring. Touting Scott's virtues of a college education and a good job, she reminds Rosemarie that they have much in common, to which Rosemarie retorts that they only have deafness in common. In desperation, Rosemarie's mother reminds her that Drew's first love is his music, "his whole life is ears," and that Rosemarie could never share that love. However, in the end, they do find happiness together, she as a dancer and he as a successful entertainer.

In spite of the fact that the film continues the tradition against deaf couples, the subject is discussed openly for the first time; and the juxtaposition of the mother, who is cold, inadequate in her communication, and willing to take advantage of Rosemarie's deafness, with her role as advocate in behalf of deaf couples is brilliant (in any previous film treatment, the mother would have been delighted for her deaf child to find a hearing mate). Unfortunately, *Voices,* described by a *New York Times* film reviewer as the best of several love stories of disability and a dream,[5] became caught up in a boycott. Marcella Meyer, a prominent deaf community leader and the executive director of the Greater Los Angeles Council on Deafness, complained that *Voices* did not have a

deaf actress in the role of Rosemarie;[6] and an Oakland-based coalition
of deaf people and friends organized a boycott of the captioned version
of *Voices,* being shown at commercial theaters in the San Francisco-
Oakland area.[7] MGM defended itself by pointing out that the film was
authentic, that it was the first studio to provide a captioned print for
commercial theaters, and that the film had employed deaf actors. However, the producer, Joe Wizman, and the director, Robert Markowitz,
claimed that they could not find a young deaf actress to play the role,[8]
which of course was not credible with the deaf community. Deaf
people knew that there were many capable deaf actors and that deaf
dancers had performed professionally as long ago as vaudeville.[9]

The next decade saw only three motion pictures that deal with deafness: *Eyes of a Stranger* (dist. Warner, 1981); *Amy* (Disney, 1981); and
Children of a Lesser God (Paramount, 1986). *Eyes of a Stranger* portrays another attractive deaf-blind-mute, the victim of a rapist. The
film stars Lauren Tewes as a Miami television anchorwoman who becomes increasingly concerned about reports of a violent rapist in the
south Florida area. The basis of her concern is the guilt she feels about
her deaf-blind-mute sister, with whom she shares an apartment. As a
young schoolgirl, she did not pay any attention to Tracy, who became
deaf, mute, and blind after being abducted. As the story unfolds, Tracy
(played by Jennifer Jason Leigh) is an attractive young woman who
manages the apartment while her sister, Jane, works; they communicate with signs and finger spelling.

Jane suspects that a man who lives in their apartment complex is the
rapist. She places an anonymous telephone call to him and tells him
she knows he is guilty. Later, he recognizes her voice on the television
news and visits her apartment, where he finds Tracy and assaults her.
The attack triggers the return of her senses, and she wounds the man
with a pistol that Jane purchased earlier. As she is looking at herself in
the mirror, she is attacked again by the wounded rapist, but then is
saved when Jane returns and shoots the man in the head. Not only is
there repetition of the *Esther Costello* surprise ending of the 1950s, but
the film characterizes deaf-blind persons as superheroes and -heroines,
and in doing so unfairly misleads the general public.[10]

The motion picture *Amy* features several deaf children in this story
of a teacher, played by Jenny Agutter, who tries to establish an articulation (speech and lip-reading) program at a residential school for deaf
children. As such, the film is both interesting and deceptive. The story

centers on a historical premise that, at the turn of the century, both society at large and schools for the deaf advocated that deaf persons could not be assimilated into the general society of hearing persons. A new teacher, Amy, who has run away from her husband in Boston, establishes classes in speech and lip-reading, giving much of her attention to one deaf boy, Henry. The school superintendent, played by Lou Fant, supports her efforts and tries to convince the school board to provide additional funds for articulation programs. The school matron, Malvina (played by Nanette Fabray), opposes Amy's efforts, arguing that deaf persons cannot learn to speak: "They need to stay with their own kind. That is their reality. Words will give them nothing but heartache and frustration—false hope. I don't want my babies to leave here with hopes that can never be realized."

Her colleagues are unaware that Amy had a deaf son who died in an asylum, which explains why she is convinced of the need to bring deaf children out of residential institutions. With the aid of a local doctor, played by Barry Newman, she organizes a school football team, which manages to defeat the local hearing school team. Finally, Malvina drops her opposition when she realizes that Henry wants to learn to speak so that he can communicate with his blind mother, who cannot see his sign language. In the interim, Amy's husband arrives to take her home, but Amy knows now that she can teach deaf children to speak and she decides to stay at the school.

The film appears to provide a balanced view of deafness, and its depiction of deaf children and sign language seems positive. One film reviewer observed that "the film's actors seem suffused with a rare humanity. Then you look closely at the actors: the deaf children all are from the California School for the Deaf in Riverside. . . . Otto Rechenberg, who so glowingly plays Henry, signs in both German and English. Lou Fant, the memorable school superintendent, is of deaf parents, a founding member of the National Theatre of the Deaf. Nanette Fabray's career has flourished in spite of a hearing loss."[11] Yet the context of the film is historically flawed and leaves viewers with a sense of triumph, implying that successful articulation programs encourage the integration of deaf persons into the mainstream of American life. Audiences are unaware that the attractive oralist Amy, like the real oralist superintendent Howard M. McManaway of the Virginia School for the Deaf in the 1930s,[12] is a pejorative symbol to the deaf community, which blamed oralists for many of the difficulties deaf people encounter. Oralists have been charged, in their pedagogical insistence that deaf children speak and read lips, with abuse of and discrimination against deaf persons as human beings. In the context of 1981, when there were many voices clamoring for the right of disabled children to be educated in mainstream schools and assimilated as adults into the society at large, *Amy* appears to present a historical view of the origins of the speech and lip-reading programs that would enable deaf persons to be integrated. However, movie theater audiences had so far seen only idealized deaf people.

Aside from a background scene in *Voices* that depicts a group of deaf adults silently signing to each other, moviegoers have no basis for suspecting the existence of an active, healthy deaf community. *Amy* posits a parochial, unassimilated, and unspeaking deaf community, which in fact does not exist in the historical film repertoire of Hollywood. It is possible that the filmmakers were reflecting accurately a cultural bias of audiences unfamiliar with real deaf persons—a bias that presumes that it is wrong for deaf people to prefer association with other deaf people; hence, the film only needed to demonstrate the importance and success of speech. Audiences reason that the absent and undepicted deaf community is inferior because they share the prevalent pejorative and pathological view of deafness and deaf persons.

The most recent film of the 1980s to deal with deafness, *Children of a Lesser God,* responded directly to complaints by the deaf community about Hollywood's failure to cast deaf actors in roles of deaf characters. Now, for the first time in sixty years, filmmakers cast a deaf actor in a major role;[13] in fact, deaf persons played all of the film's deaf characters. Though an important achievement, clearly Hollywood could have done no less without risking a tremendous outpouring of rage from the deaf community.

Children of a Lesser God, written by Mark Medoff, first appeared as a stage play in Los Angeles and eventually on Broadway, where it earned recognition through the reception of several Tony Awards.[14] From the deaf community's perspective, the most important award went to deaf actress Phyllis Frelich for her performance in the leading role of Sarah. Thereafter, the play toured major cities throughout the United States, where it met an enthusiastic reception. In each touring company production, deaf actors played the roles of deaf characters, so it is most improbable that the filmmakers could have cast hearing actors in these roles.

From the outset the film version received enthusiastic support. Reviewers provided positive critiques and identified the leading actors, William Hurt and Marlee Matlin, as probable nominees for Academy Awards.[15] Regardless of this aura of success, the film exemplifies the previous history of the depiction of deafness in the movies: in spite of the fact that a major character is deaf, deafness itself is deemphasized. Advertisements for the film followed the same pattern established for *Johnny Belinda*—there was no information about deafness. Shortly after its initial appearance, several newspaper and magazine stories about *Children of a Lesser God* emphasized that the film is a love story, and some film reviewers, as well as the film's director, Randa Haines, contended that the movie represents an improvement over the stage play since the filmmakers eliminated "deaf politics" in favor of the love story.[16]

In the film version, the story concentrates on the struggle of James Leeds (Hurt), a speech teacher, and Sarah Norman (Matlin), a deaf cleaning woman, to understand and respect each other. In the beginning James only wants to know why Sarah refuses to speak and why she is suspicious of his attention to her. In time he learns that "hearing" boys pursued her only for purposes of sex: they did not bother to learn how to communicate with her; they did not even "buy her a coke, first." Though they do not fully understand each other's world, James and Sarah become lovers and she moves in with him. Each is good at what he or she does. There are marvelous scenes in which James taps his high school students' natural interests to improve their speech. He teaches them to sing-sign popular music and rhythms; he even teaches a basketball player how to articulate the obscenities "fuck-face" and "asshole." For her part, Sarah resolves to do only those things she does well: she is a good cleaning woman and a good bed partner.

Recognizing her intelligence as well as her beauty, James is convinced that Sarah could be successful if she would learn to speak, though this is a topic he has promised her he will avoid. Neither fits into the other's world: James's hearing colleagues attribute Sarah's poker-playing skill to his tutelage and perhaps some nonverbal cheating; and at a party of mostly deaf people, James is shut out of the rapid-fire signed conversations. The party results in a crisis for the lovers. Sarah is upset by the evidence that a nonspeaking deaf person—the guest of honor—can complete a doctorate and find successful professional employment. Blaming James for her failure to achieve an identity, she tries to explain her feelings through the metaphor of the ASL sign "to connect." Angered by her accusation that he only sees her as "deaf," James accuses her of hiding behind her deafness and forces her to speak. When she does, he realizes that Sarah has terrible speech.

Sarah runs away to her mother and tries to find an identity separate from James. While she is gone, James continues to try to understand her deafness, her world of silence. He even returns to the underwater world of the school swimming pool, which is a metaphor of Sarah's silence, yet fails to come to a full understanding. Sarah, however, realizes that she loves James and can achieve her identity with him, and so she returns to the school, where they reconcile. They both recognize that they cannot fully understand or enter each other's world but that they can share a relationship somewhere in the middle, that they can "connect."

Like society at large, Hollywood refuses to acknowledge and thereby depict the scope and nature of the problem of deafness. When the film reduces the scale of the conflict to one between Sarah and James, it virtually eliminates any possibility that a movie audience will understand the larger cultural discrimination with which deaf persons contend.

In the stage play, there is a deaf character, Orin Dennis, who fights for the civil rights of deaf persons. He hires an attorney to file a complaint with an employment commission against the school where Sarah worked as a cleaning woman. Sarah decides to appear as a witness because she does not want the attorney or any other hearing person to speak for deaf people. She writes her own speech. In the interim, James goes to the school superintendent and works out an agreement whereby the school will hire deaf professionals if the complaint is dropped. Sarah is offended that James would act for deaf people and leaves him.[17] The play ends with the two lovers separated but expressing the hope that they will come back together to help each other grow, to share.

The centerpiece in the sequence of events is Sarah's speech, prepared for the commission. In it, Sarah uses the sign "to connect" to express the concept that two individuals can be joined in a shared relationship—one relationship with two individual lives: "I want to be joined to other people, but for all my life people have spoken for me: She says; she means; she wants. As if there were no I. As if there were no one in here who could understand. Until you let me be an individual, an I, just as you are, you will never truly be able to come inside my silence and know me. And until you can do that, I will never let myself know you. Until that time, we cannot be joined. We cannot share a relationship."[18] In the film, this speech is directed at James and the dialogue about the discrimination is dropped completely. The audience is exposed to powerful acting through a script reduced to the essential love story.

Undoubtedly, the film finally allows audiences to recognize the power and beauty of sign language, something no other motion picture has done quite as well, even in the silent film era. The deaf actor Granville Redmond had communicated only in limited signs in one film, and audiences generally saw deaf persons and ASL only in background scenes. Hearing actors who had played deaf characters simply were incapable of sustained and substantive dialogue in sign language. But Marlee Matlin and other members of the deaf cast of *Children of a Lesser God* broke this barrier, though at the expense of "deaf politics."

From a deaf person's perspective, the film includes surprising technical flaws. To ensure that hearing audiences would understand Sarah's signs, the filmmakers borrowed the technique used in *Johnny Belinda* and have James interpret or respond appropriately to her dialogue. Yet the camera routinely cuts off Sarah's signs and the lighting often obscures their visibility, so that deaf persons cannot always follow the signed dialogue. Even if such decisions were based on the director's notion of artistic imagery, these faults could have been compensated for through the provision of open captions. They were not.

The film's distribution has adhered to the now traditional path of segregated viewing for deaf audiences. Here is a film of major importance to the deaf community, but there are only limited captioned versions. When the film opened at movie theaters in the Washington, D.C., area, home of Gallaudet University, where many of the American deaf actors had received their higher education and drama training, there was only one theater that provided captioned versions and only at limited viewing times. This pattern has been replicated in major cities throughout the United States; and deaf persons who live in many cities simply have no opportunity to see a captioned version in a movie theater. It is possible that film distributors dismissed this limited access as further evidence of "deaf politics"; however, the deaf community understands that this is one more example of discrimination that has become routine for deaf persons.

NOTES

(For film documentation, see the Filmography.)

1. In *The Films of Anthony Quinn* (Secaucus, N.J.: Citadel Press, 1975), Alvin H. Marill observes that this low-budget film failed to earn back its costs and that, whereas the role permitted Quinn to mime for the first time in his career, it primarily gave the star "a quick two weeks pay between assignments" (p. 244). MGM publicity releases identified Deaf Smith as a Civil War veteran who fought with Sam Houston's forces against Santa Anna— although the Civil War occurred nearly three decades after the Texas wars. See *"Deaf Smith and Johnny Ears:* MGM Pressbook," C–37, Motion Picture Division, Library of Congress (hereafter, LC). For further discussion of this historical figure, see *Martyrs of the Alamo* (1915) in the Filmography.

2. For an excellent discussion of auteur theory and the imprint of directors Richard Brooks and Robert Altman on *Looking for Mr. Goodbar* and *Nashville,* respectively, see Robin Wood, *Hollywood from Vietnam to Reagan* (New York: Columbia University Press, 1986) , pp. 11–14, 26–31, 55–58.

3. *Wall Street Journal* (March 31, 1975), p. 11, in *"Tommy:* Clippings," Academy of Motion Picture Arts and Sciences (hereafter, AMPAS).

4. In fact, in Judith Rossner's novel, Theresa was simply a schoolteacher. See the discussion in Wood, *Hollywood,* p. 56.

5. *New York Times* (March 14, 1979), III, 22:3.

6. Quoted in "Films of Deaf Not for Deaf," *Los Angeles Times* (March 14, 1979), in *"Voices:* Clippings," AMPAS. Meyer also complained that certain television movies dealing with deafness were not captioned.

7. See *Variety* (June 8, 1979), in *"Voices:* Clippings," AMPAS.

8. See *"Voices:* MGM Press Release, May 1979," AMPAS.

9. Louis Weinberg (stage name David Marvel) was a deaf dancer who also appeared in the silent film *The Woman Who God Forgot* (Artcraft-Paramount, 1917). See also Jerry Flail, "Florita: Dancing Star," *The Silent Worker* (March 1949), p. 5; and an article on Charles and Charlotte Lamberton: Harry Taub, "They Danced Their Way to Fame," *The Silent News* (August 1973), p. 9.

10. See Carol Yoken, *Living with Deaf-Blindness: Nine Profiles* (Washington, D.C.: National Academy of Gallaudet College, 1979), p. 1. For a more positive analysis of this film, see Wood, *Hollywood,* pp. 198–201.

11. *Los Angeles Times* (April 10, 1981), in *"Amy:* Clippings," AMPAS.

12. McManaway, a staunch oralist, administered the Virginia School for

the Deaf and Blind and in 1930 became president of the American Association to Promote the Teaching of Speech to the Deaf. He and Reuben I. Altizer (see n. 22 in the Introduction) locked horns throughout the 1930s in a protracted oral-manual controversy that resulted in McManaway's resignation and Altizer's becoming editor and publisher of *The Silent Cavalier,* an influential deaf community newspaper.

13. The previous and only appearance of a deaf actor in a major role was the silent film actor Granville Redmond in *You'd Be Surprised* (Paramount, 1926).

14. For the early history of the play, see Mark Medoff, "Introduction," *Children of a Lesser God, a Play in Two Acts* (Clifton, N.J.: James T. White Co., 1980), pp. vii-xix.

15. For example, see Paul Attanasio, "The Soundless Love of 'Lesser God,'" *Washington Post* (October 3, 1986), D-1, D-8; Rita Kempley, "'Lesser God': Greater Love," *Washington Post Weekend Magazine* (October 3, 1986), p. 27. Matlin won an Oscar for best actress.

16. See Paul Attanasio, "Randa Haines' Inner Voice," *Washington Post* (October 12, 1986), F-1, F-5.

17. The scene appears in its entirety in Medoff, *Children,* pp. 68–85.

18. Ibid., p. 84.

5

The Impact of Television

The deaf community has a long-standing interest in television. In the late 1920s, *The Frat* began featuring articles that discussed the new technology of television. An article entitled "Modern Inventions and the Deaf," reprinted from the *Kansas Star*, pointed out that sound technology (movies and radio) and the telephone had created problems for deaf people but that "the more sanguine prophets predict a time when television would enable the deaf to use the spelled or signed word at great distances. . . . thus the deaf look expectantly to these new inventions, knowing that they are not altogether deprived of their benefits."[1]

The Great Depression and World War II postponed the widespread implementation of television technology until the early fifties, when it became evident that, as far as deaf viewers were concerned, television would be yet one more technological disappointment. A recent chronicler of events in the deaf community observed that: ". . . most television programs were just another form of the 'talkies' and were meaningless to anyone who could not understand the dialogue. Even the most skilled lipreaders could catch only scattered bits of information when a speaker's lips happened to be clearly visible on the screen."[2] When advances did occur in television, they took place at the local station level and most often involved the inclusion of interpreters in locally produced religious or news broadcasts. Early prime-time national network television entertainment programs easily matched Hollywood's output of scripts depicting deafness or deaf characters: at its peak in the 1950s, Hollywood produced thirteen such films, while the national television networks carried nineteen programs with deaf characters.[3]

In *TV: The Most Popular Art*, Horace Newcomb observes that television formulas require the use of ". . . contemporary historical concerns as subject matter."[4] Many of the television shows depicting deafness confirm Newcomb's observation. "Racket Squad: His Brother's Keeper" (CBS, 1953) deals with charity solicitation and deaf imposters; "Big Town: Mute Justice" (CBS, 1954) depicts a deaf-mute, deprived of compensation from an accident and victimized by his unscrupulous interpreter; and "Big Story: Born—A Son" (NBC, 1955) and "The Listening Hand" (ABC, 1956) report on the efforts of an Ohio social work agency to gain custody of the newborn child of a deaf-blind couple. Several other programs took advantage of the new hearing aid technology to dramatize "missed opportunities": Merle Oberon fails to hear her husband plot to kill her in "Four Star Playhouse: Sound Off, My Love" (CBS, 1953), and Nancy Malone fails to hear a marriage proposal in "Robert Montgomery Presents: There's No Need to Shout" (NBC, 1955); both women eventually overcome their vanity and don hearing aids. "Medic: My Very Good Friend Albert" (NBC, 1954) represents the ability of the medical show genre to tap quickly into deafness as a medical problem. The program discusses otosclerosis and fenestration operations, which Liberace submitted to in the Hollywood musical *Sincerely Yours* (1955).

Like the stereotyped deaf characters of motion pictures, most "deaf" characters in dramatic television shows of the fifties and sixties reflect the same stereotypes. Two national network programs in 1957 depicted the familiar characters: the mute dummy, in "Schlitz Playhouse: The Life You Save," and the naturally speaking lip-reader in "Loretta Young Show: Double Partners."

The widely publicized "The Life You Save" features the prominent dancer-actor Gene Kelly, in his first dramatic television appearance, as a one-armed tramp named Tom Triplet who offers to fix things at Mrs. Craigie's farm in exchange for room and board. Mrs. Craigie (played by Agnes Moorehead) realizes that Triplet is both competent (he repairs her car) and charming (he teaches her deaf-mute daughter, Lucynell [played by Janice Rule], to say her first word, "birdt") and convinces him to marry the "angelic" Lucynell, "who can't talk back." Immediately after the wedding, Triplet regrets his decision and, once safely away from Mrs. Craigie, abandons his bride at a roadside café and heads down the highway in the car he repaired. When he sees a sign that reads "The Life You Save May Be Your Own," he repents and soon after he returns for Lucynell. She is so grateful that she articulates her second word, "Tom." In addition to the traditional use of speech as

a measure of success for adult deaf-mute characters, the program reinforces the image of a deaf person as victim, with the contrasting
image of the amputee as both competent and charming.[5]

In "Double Partners," Loretta Young plays a deaf wife, Ruth Baxter,
who is her husband's partner in a law practice. When a private investigator named Planchek (whose lips she cannot read because he speaks
with a foreign accent) is killed in her office, Ruth is determined to track
down the murderer. Her chief suspect is a crooked politician who conducts his business on a park bench below her law office window; she
uses binoculars to read his lips. The politician tests Ruth's hearing by
dropping a soda-pop bottle behind her, supposedly proving she is deaf
and therefore could not have heard anything that might incriminate
him; the test, of course, only confirms Ruth's suspicions. Unfortunately, her hearing husband refuses to believe that the politician is corrupt and thwarts her efforts, but at program's end, he realizes his error
and saves Ruth from being killed.[6]

Alfred Hitchcock also used this more common stereotype—the perfect lip-reader and naturally speaking deaf character—as a surprise
element in the climax of "Alfred Hitchcock Presents: You Got to Have
Luck" (CBS, 1956). The villain in the show (John Cassavetes) terrorizes a housewife (Marisa Pavan), hitting her when she turns on the
radio too loud and forcing her to give dictated answers in response to
a telephone call. When he leaves the house, he is surprised by waiting
policemen and discovers that the housewife, who spoke clearly, was
really deaf and had been reading his lips. The telephone caller, who
had expected to speak with the husband, the usual telephone respon-
dent, suspected that the wife was in danger and had called the police.[7]
Hitchcock was able to capitalize on the fact that audiences would be
surprised by a deaf character who behaves as a hearing person yet
would find the result plausible.

Other traditional treatments of deaf characters appeared in what has
become known, in hindsight, as the golden age of live television: two
nationally broadcast teleplays of *Johnny Belinda*, starring Katherine
Bard in 1955 and Julie Harris in 1958; and Teresa Wright as Anne
Sullivan and Patty McCormick as Helen Keller in the 1957 "Playhouse
90" teleplay of *The Miracle Worker*. These stereotypes persisted
throughout the next three decades, along with the practice, continued
from motion pictures, of casting hearing actors as deaf characters.

(The deaf actress Audree Norton's 1968 appearance on an episode of "Mannix: The Silent Cry" proved the exception to the rule.[8])

The seventies marked a breakthrough in access to television for deaf viewers as captioning started to catch on. Although television had made occasional use of both sign-language interpretation and captioning, the latter now became the focus of the deaf community leadership.

Sign-language interpretation is simple, flexible, and cheap. However, it is often imprecise and hard to read when reduced to a small corner of the television screen. Some local television stations chose instead to hire deaf newscasters, who signed and usually had understandable but real deaf voices. In 1972, for example, San Francisco's KRON-TV hired Jane Wilk and Peter Wechsberg as deaf broadcasters of an early morning news show, "Newsign."[9] A few other stations followed suit, in communities scattered across the United States, but at the national network level the debate centered on captioning.

Unlike the relatively unregulated film industry, television stations depend upon broadcast licenses issued by the Federal Communications Commission (FCC). Throughout the fifties and sixties, deaf viewers complained about the absence of captions, particularly when stations broadcast notices of emergencies in the community, such as for tornadoes and blizzards. In response to these complaints, the FCC, in 1970, suggested that television stations use captioned emergency notices. When there was no notable response to the FCC suggestion, a group of George Washington University law students formed an organization known as Deafwatch and filed a petition with the FCC to require emergency captions on all television stations. In 1975 the FCC issued such an order.[10]

Underlying the order was the general issue of captions for deaf viewers, and the early discussion focused on open- versus closed-captions. Although the networks believed that hearing viewers would object to open-captions, which everyone could see, the ABC network captioned its late evening news program in the fall of 1973 (which forced deaf viewers to stay up late or miss out on the news of the day). At the same time, the PBS network developed closed-captioned technology, which restricts the appearance of captions to television receivers equipped with special decoders. The devices make use of a part of the television broadcast signal that does not normally appear on the screen, popularly known as line 21. Despite network objections, the FCC granted PBS access to line 21 for captions in 1976, and when access was reaffirmed in 1979, ABC, NBC, and finally CBS agreed to join PBS in the closed-captioned technology. The National Captioning Institute, established the following year, became responsible for the creation of captions, as well as the selection of programs for captioning. Hence, by 1980, a federally approved "separate but equal" philosophy of television entertainment became a fact of life for deaf viewers.[11]

In contrast to the separatist direction that captioned films and television programs had taken, federal laws and regulations enacted during the seventies resulted in mainstreaming disabled children, particularly the mentally retarded, into the nation's public schools. Much of the impetus for this can be attributed to the success of several lawsuits, including, in 1971, *Pennsylvania Association for Retarded Children* v. *Commonwealth of Pennsylvania* and *Mills* v. *Board of Education* (Washington, D.C.). Special educators have argued that these judicial principles should be applied to all disabled children, which of course includes deaf students. Section 504 of the Rehabilitation Act of 1973 and the Education for All Handicapped Children Act of 1975 (P.L. 94–142) have raised public consciousness about disability and have fostered debate about the precise meaning of these acts. In varying degrees, a more politically astute National Association of the Deaf (NAD) has participated in these activities—in fact, in 1976 it established a legal defense fund in support of antidiscrimination litigation on behalf of the deaf community.[12]

In particular, the NAD has focused its attention on two issues: total communication, and the employment of deaf administrators in education and rehabilitation programs. Simply stated, *total communication,* a term invented by a deaf teacher and school administrator named Roy K. Holcomb, represents a pedagogical approach to deaf children that emphasizes speech, lip-reading, aural amplification, finger spelling, and signs, and varies according to the needs of the individual. In effect, this combined approach tries to bridge the old gap between sign advocates and oral advocates. The NAD has long argued that educators of deaf children should look to the deaf adult community for advice and guidance, since they are the products of earlier school systems. To this end, the NAD has actively campaigned for the hiring of deaf individuals, particularly in the fields of education and rehabilitation. Holcomb, who has implemented his total communication program in a public school in Santa Ana, California, is one of several deaf persons who earned appointments to top administrative positions during the seventies.[13]

Within this milieu of increased sensitivity to and participation of disabled citizens in the society at large, national television networks, in the 1970s, carried more than twenty entertainment programs featuring major or pivotal deaf characters. These included "Baretta: Shoes" (ABC, 1976), featuring mutes, and naturally speaking lip-readers in "Lassie: A Joyous Sound" (CBS, 1973). Medical shows dealt with hysterical deafness, in "Medical Center: Wall of Silence" (CBS, 1973), and with deaf persons having a family history of deafness but who could benefit from modern surgical techniques, in "Marcus Welby, M.D.: Child of Silence" (ABC, 1975) and "Westside Medical: The Sound of Sunlight" (ABC, 1977). Although children, women, and Indians had been cast as deaf characters, television audiences saw the first black deaf adults appear as a successful machine shop owner, in "Good Times" (CBS, 1975), and as an illiterate mute dockworker accused of rape in the television movie *Dummy* (CBS, 1979). Other contemporary issues, such as the effort of a deaf couple to adopt their hearing foster child and the effort of a profoundly deaf student to mainstream in a regular public high school, are depicted in "The Man and the City: Hands of Love" (CBS, 1971) and "James at 15: Actions Speak Louder" (NBC, 1978).

Four made-for-television movies in 1979 presented all of the deaf stereotypes: *And Your Name Is Jonah* (CBS); *Dummy* (CBS); *The Miracle Worker* (NBC); and *Silent Victory: The Kitty O'Neill Story* (CBS). Patty Duke Astin added an Emmy Award for her television portrayal of Anne Sullivan to her earlier Academy Award for her 1962 film role as the young Helen Keller in *The Miracle Worker*. Melissa Gilbert, from the popular "Little House on the Prairie" series, plays the deaf-blind girl who emerges from darkness through repeated finger spelling. *Silent Victory*, the true story of a deaf stuntwoman and driver who held several athletic and world land speed records, presents the lip-reader with perfect speech. Stockard Channing portrays Kitty O'Neill in her struggle to break away from her mother in order to pursue an independent career. O'Neill owed her communication skills to her mother, played by Colleen Dewhurst, who told her as a two-year-old, when she was diagnosed as deaf, "You will never use sign language, Kitty O'Neill. You will learn to hear with your eyes and speak to others as they speak to you."

In *Dummy*, based on a true story, we find two deaf characters: the dummy, Donald Lang (played by LeVar Burton), a black dockworker who has no understandable method of communication and is accused of the murder of a prostitute; and Lowell Myers (played by Paul Sorvino), a white deaf attorney who can communicate in signs and finger spelling but prefers to read lips and use his own speech-impaired voice. The constitutional question presented is whether a deaf person who is legally incompetent, unable to understand the accusation against him, and unable to assist in his own defense, can be incarcerated in jail or in a mental institution if he is not mentally ill but simply illiterate and unable to communicate.

Initially held in a mental institution, Lang is released and ordered to stand trial. With Myers's help he is finally freed for lack of evidence, only to be arrested when a second prostitute is found dead. The story ends with Lang being sentenced to the Cook County jail. A secondary story line deals with Myers's concern about his deteriorating voice, the result of a progressive hearing loss. Although a couple of deaf characters had been allowed to use their voices in earlier shows, Myers was the first major deaf character to do so. In fact, the entire story is told from Myers's point of view, since Lang cannot communicate; thus the audience continually hears his speech-impaired voice. As such, this portrayal represents a significant departure from the predominant stereotypes of mutes and perfect speakers.

And Your Name Is Jonah stars Sally Struthers as Mrs. Corelli, who, in her efforts to find help for her deaf son, Jonah (played by Jeffrey Bravin), encounters conflicting advice from the experts and learns that not all deaf children are able to speak or read lips. After her husband (James Woods) abandons the family, and Jonah remains as uncommunicative as ever, she meets a deaf couple, quite by chance, who introduce her to other deaf adults. For the first time Mrs. Corelli is exposed to sign language, and her new deaf friends are able to achieve communication with Jonah by teaching him that his favorite delicacy, a hot dog, has a sign. Mrs. Corelli enrolls him in a program that uses "total communication," and at movie's end Jonah tells a little girl, "My name is Jonah."

Aside from issues of stereotype or communication methodology, the movie is unique because all of the deaf characters are played by real deaf persons (including Barbara Bernstein and Bernard Bragg as the

National Theatre of the Deaf alumna Linda Bove appeared as deaf character Melissa Haley on the television soap opera "Search for Tomorrow" (NBC, initial appearance in 1973). Courtesy of Laura-Jean Gilbert.

Deaf cast members *(left to right)* Phyllis Frelich, Julianna Fjeld, and Ed Waterstreet, with Sid Caesar *(center),* from the Emmy award-winning movie *Love Is Never Silent* (NBC, Hallmark Hall of Fame, 1985). Courtesy of Julianna Fjeld.

Deaf actors Phyllis Frelich and Ed Waterstreet as the deaf parents in *Love Is Never Silent*. Courtesy of Gallaudet University Archives.

(Top, left to right): Ed Waterstreet, Phyllis Frelich, Lou Fant, and Julianna Fjeld, of *Love Is Never Silent,* finger spell "ex-NTD." Courtesy of Julianna Fjeld. *(Bottom):* Deaf actress Jane Norman *(left)* interviews Julianna Fjeld, Emmy award-winning executive producer of *Love Is Never Silent.* Courtesy of Gallaudet University Archives.

(Top): On the set of "NBC Experiment in Television" (1967), the first televised appearance of the actors who formed the National Theatre of the Deaf—*(left to right)* Audree Norton, Arthur Penn, June Russi Eastman, Howard Palmer, Phyllis Frelich, Lou Fant, and Ralph White. Courtesy of Gilbert Eastman. *(Bottom):* Phyllis Frelich, winner of a Tony Award, as the original Sarah in the stage play *Children of a Lesser God,* in 1979. Courtesy of Gallaudet University Archives.

Marlee Matlin receives an honorary doctorate from Gallaudet University. She was the first deaf person to be awarded an Oscar by the film entertainment industry, for her portrayal of Sarah in *Children of a Lesser God* (Paramount, 1986). Courtesy of Gallaudet University Archives.

deaf couple, and Billy Seago as Jonah's sign-language teacher). This had become a burning issue in the deaf community. Unlike the motion picture industry, which literally had not hired a deaf actor since the days of silent film, television had begun to open doors of opportunity to deaf actors. For example, in addition to her "Mannix" role, Audree Norton appeared in episodes of "Family Affair," "The Man and the City," and "Streets of San Francisco." National Theatre of the Deaf alumna Linda Bove has a recurring role on the popular children's educational program "Sesame Street" and was on television's longest-running daytime serial "Search for Tomorrow." Another deaf actor, Kevin Van Wieringer, played a deaf soccer player who mainstreams into a public high school in an episode of "James at 15." And June Reed, a student at the Mary Bennett School for the Deaf in Los Angeles, the first deaf child actor, appeared in "Ben Casey: A Woods Full of Question Marks" (NBC, 1964) three years before the first appearance of deaf adult actors, as part of the newly formed NTD, on an NBC "Special."

In 1978 and 1979 a controversy involving Audree Norton convinced many persons in the deaf community that both the movie and television industries discriminated against deaf actors. The ABC network had created a series of bimonthly shows, "ABC Afterschool Specials," designed for young adolescents, and by the late seventies they commanded nearly a quarter of the afternoon viewing audience.[14] In 1978, scriptwriters prepared a story about the efforts of a hearing teenager to cope with her feelings of shame about her deaf parents. Since Audree Norton had played the role of a deaf mother who wanted to adopt a hearing foster child in the 1971 production of "Man and the City: Hands of Love," it was natural for her and her deaf husband to audition for the role of the deaf parents in "ABC Afterschool Special: Mom and Dad Can't Hear Me." Norton reported that the casting director told her that "of all the people, you and your husband won the roles. But you are out because the director is afraid to use deaf actors and actresses. He prefers to use speaking actors and actresses." The program's producer, Daniel Wilson, denied the accusation and stated that hearing actors Priscilla Pointer and Stephen Elliott were "right" for the parts and that producers should not limit themselves to deaf actors for deaf roles.[15] Although Norton filed a complaint with the Screen Actors Guild in San Francisco, the guild's national headquarters in Los Angeles accepted the explanation provided by Wilson. Soon the complaint escalated to a generalized protest by deaf persons on the West Coast.

If one compares the number of appearances by deaf actors on national network television in the 1970s and 1980s, it is apparent that the protest in 1979 made a significant difference. Although Audree Norton apparently personally bore the brunt of any negative reaction from the industry, since she did not again work in television after her grievance, the overall number of appearances by deaf actors in the 1980s has increased dramatically. From 1970 through 1979 there were at least thirty-four readily identifiable deaf characters on network television; deaf actors performed in eleven of these roles, or approximately 33 percent. From 1980 through 1986 there have been twenty-four corresponding roles, of which eighteen, or approximately 75 percent, were performed by deaf actors. By any standard this is a tremendous change and represents a major breakthrough in the historical employment practices of the industry.

Although notable exceptions continue to appear, the programs of the 1980s reflect a more complex view of deafness and deaf persons.[16] The popular comedy series "Barney Miller" featured a 1981 episode that depicts the arrest of a deaf prostitute. While awaiting the arrival of her deaf attorney and her deaf pimp, the prostitute, played by Tony Award-winner Phyllis Frelich, charms her arresting officer and they arrange to meet for a Chinese dinner. Deaf actors play all the deaf character roles, and in thirty minutes of humor the story introduces audiences to new and varied perspectives of deafness.

The 1980s marked another achievement for deaf persons when a major television movie featuring deafness received an Emmy Award. The Hallmark Hall of Fame production of *Love Is Never Silent* (NBC, 1985) won recognition as the best drama of the year. Adapted from Joanne Greenberg's novel, *In This Sign* (1970), the film tells the story of a deaf couple raising hearing children prior to World War II. Frelich and deaf actor Ed Waterstreet play the deaf couple. Another deaf member of the cast, Julianna Fjeld, achieved a breakthrough in that she owned the film rights to the original novel and served as a producer of the teleplay.[17] When she took her place at the podium, along with her interpreter, to accept her Emmy, she symbolized the hope expressed in 1929 that television would compensate for the loss the deaf community experienced when the movie industry abandoned the technology of silent films. Television has not met all of the expectations of deaf people, but it certainly has come a long way since its initial popularity in the 1950s, and it certainly is more accessible than motion pictures.

NOTES

(For film documentation, see the Filmography.)

1. Quoted in *The Silent Worker* (February 1929), p. 102. See also *The Frat* (January 1929), pp. 4–5; *Deaf-Mutes' Journal* (January 17, 1929), p. 2.

2. Jack R. Gannon, *Deaf Heritage: A Narrative History of Deaf America* (Silver Spring, Md.: National Association of the Deaf, 1981), p. 385.

3. See ibid., pp. 193, 262, 384–90 for a survey of television and the deaf community. For specific film titles or episodes, consult the Filmography.

4. Horace Newcomb, *TV: The Most Popular Art* (Garden City, N.Y.: Anchor Books, 1974), p. 19.

5. "The Life You Save: Synopsis," Copyright Registration, LP 8365, Motion Picture, Broadcasting, and Recorded Sound Division, Library of Congress (hereafter, LC).

6. "Double Partners: Script," Copyright Registration, LP 9625, LC.

7. "You Got to Have Luck: Synopsis," Copyright Registration, LP 6791, LC.

8. In 1968, the same year as the release of *Psych-Out* and *The Heart Is a Lonely Hunter,* Norton appeared in an episode of the popular television detective series. This marked the first time in thirty-seven years that a professionally trained deaf actor had been employed in a role in a commercially produced film or television program since silent film actor Granville Redmond appeared in Charlie Chaplin's *City Lights.* In 1967 a group of deaf actors appeared on "NBC Special: Experiment in Television" to promote the existence and forthcoming national tour of the newly created National Theatre of the Deaf.

9. See Gregg Brooks, "A TV First . . . News for the Deaf by Deaf Newscasters," *Deaf American* (July-August 1972), pp. 3–4. For a general discussion of television, see the entire issue of "Television and the Deaf," *Gallaudet Today* (Winter 1973). For a discussion of the advantages and disadvantages of sign-language interpreting versus captions, see Jerome D. Schein and Ronald N. Hamilton, *Impact, 1980: Telecommunication and Deafness* (Silver Spring, Md.: National Association of the Deaf, 1980), pp. 11–19.

10. During this period I was the academic dean of Gallaudet University and, due to my own legal training, had the opportunity to know the key players in these events. Law professor John Banzhaf of George Washington University, assisted by attorney Glenn Goldberg, directed the activities to a successful conclusion.

11. Recently, Gary W. Olsen, the executive director of the National Association of the Deaf, spoke about captions and reminded the audience that the "total number of program hours still remain at only a small percentage when compared with the viewing options available to the general public" due to the lack of funds for increased captioning. Reprinted in "Address to the Communications Barrier Forum, National Council and the Handicapped, May 14, 1986," *The New NAD Broadcaster* (July 1986), p. 7.

12. See Sy DuBow et al., *Legal Rights of Hearing-Impaired People: National Center for Law and the Deaf* (Washington, D.C.: Gallaudet College Press, 1982).

13. See Edward L. Scouten, *Turning Points in the Education of Deaf People* (Danville, Ill.: Interstate Printers, 1984), pp. 326–30.

14. Squire D. Rushnell, "Specials and MiniSeries," in *TV and Teens, Experts Look at the Issues: Action for Children's Television,* ed. Meg Schwarz (Reading, Mass.: Addison Wesley Publishing, 1982), pp. 35–37.

15. Quoted in the Fremont, Calif., *Argus* (April 5, 1978), in "Audree Norton: Vertical Files," Collection on Deafness, Gallaudet University, Washington, D.C.

16. Poorly executed signed dialogue, accompanied by scenes that feature a deaf character with exaggerated lip-reading (through binoculars) and tactile skills, marks a recent episode of "Magnum, P.I.: One Picture Is Worth" (CBS, October 8, 1986) as an exception to the trend of general progress. Hearing actress Stephanie Dunnam plays the deaf character.

17. See "Prime Time Players: Gallaudet Graduates Star in 'Love Is Never Silent,'" *Gallaudet Today* (Spring 1986), pp. 6–8.

Conclusion

What is the Hollywood image of deafness? In her analysis of the image of women in films, Molly Haskell uses the term "the big lie" in concluding that the movie industry has served as a popular agent to foster and perpetuate the myth of women as the weaker sex.[1] Is there a comparable "big lie" in the Hollywood depiction of deaf characters? If so, one must conclude that a collective Hollywood is guilty of the perpetuation of a pathological view of deafness as a disease and of deaf individuals as abnormal. At the same time, it is only fair to observe that the film industry did not invent this perspective.

Filmmakers reflect the prevailing American cultural bias toward disability and deafness. There certainly exists a large network, both in the United States and abroad, of educational, rehabilitation, and medical professionals who are dedicated to the proposition that deaf people, particularly children, have special needs that require their expertise. Unlike the professional who can take the time to deal with the complexities represented by deafness, movies try to convey their messages as simply as possible and, in doing so, often turn to formulas and stereotypes in their depiction of deafness. It is at this level that films have so much potential for harm. More than any other medium, they have popularized simple-minded views of deafness. This survey of film and television entertainment programs clearly demonstrates that the deaf community has every right to complain about the practices of Hollywood in the industry's depiction of deafness up to the present.

Often described as the invisible handicap, deafness remains a mystery to most Americans. The motion picture industry has contributed little to a better understanding of the deaf community. Historically, Hollywood's ideal deaf person has been truly invisible—other than the inability to hear, the stereotyped movie ideal invariably speaks clearly and reads lips with unfailing accuracy—both unrealistic exaggerations. Talking motion pictures have continued the negative image of deafness established in silent films. Often, a movie ends with a cure through an experimental drug (*And Now Tomorrow*), an operation (*Flesh and Fury*), or a psychologically traumatic event (*The Story of Esther Costello*). When the character's deafness cannot be cured, the film ends with the character acquiring speech, the symbol of success for the "dumb" individual (*The Miracle Worker*). In common with the depiction of other disabled figures, the deaf character contemplates suicide (*Sincerely Yours*); and like his or her literary brethren, the deaf character often serves as a symbol for loneliness and alienation (*The Heart Is a Lonely Hunter*). Hollywood has avoided deaf couples or families, and movies very rarely have more than one deaf character. With two exceptions, in 1926 (*You'd Be Surprised*) and most recently in 1986 (*Children of a Lesser God*), actors who could hear have always played the role of deaf persons in theatrically released films. Until 1979, in the movie *Voices,* audiences had not heard real deaf speech from a deaf adult character. Only deaf children, usually portrayed by a class from nearby schools for deaf children, have difficulty with speech.

In Hollywood's view there is little or no humor in deafness. This has been particularly true since the demise of silent motion pictures. Of the more than one hundred movies and television programs produced since the advent of sound technology, only three associate a deaf character with humor.[2] Westerns and horror films constitute less than a half-dozen films involving deafness; all of the rest are melodramas. In the movie houses of America, deaf people are usually victims, either to be pitied or cured. It is clear that the Hollywood stereotypes of deaf persons as either "dummies" or "perfect lip-readers" represent the extremes, which rarely are encountered in the real world.

Deafness is a disability in a society that communicates primarily through sound and speech. Deaf persons have been killed by oncoming automobiles and trains that they could not hear, shot by policemen with whom they could not communicate easily, incarcerated in mental institutions and jailed by professionals who misunderstood and misdiagnosed them and their deafness. They have been denied equal employment opportunities by individuals who equate good speech and English skills with intelligence. It is on this aspect of deafness that Hollywood has focused its camera lens.

There is another view, however. In the past, some deaf people accepted the fact they would never hear and, as a result, developed cultural responses to a dominant hearing society that could not and would not assimilate them. At least as early as the antebellum nineteenth century, there emerged a deaf community replete with its own social organization, schools, churches, clubs, self-help societies, newspapers and magazines, and language. In spite of the fact that the American deaf community is considered to be the most independent and progressive such community in the world, and that within the United States the Los Angeles (the spiritual if not geographical center of Hollywood) deaf community is considered to be one of the most assertive and politically astute groups at the local level, the normal activities of this community are largely unknown to the public, and no movie or television script has dealt with its existence or activities at a substantive level. It is clear that the movie industry has been a primary vehicle for the transmission and perpetuation of an American cultural view that depicts deafness as a pathological condition. The deaf community does not exist in film or television, only deafness and deaf individuals do.

The reason for this is clear. Hollywood cannot or will not deal with the issue of language in the deaf community. Individual deaf characters are excellent victims. Like their blind counterparts, these characters look good; and since filmmakers value a pleasing physical appearance, this explains why deafness and blindness predominate among disabled characters in film. It is no accident that in more than eighty years of film there have been no multiply disabled deaf characters depicted, with the exception of deaf-blind portrayals (of course, the deaf-blind characters have met the test of good looks). It is only when two deaf characters appear in a film together that communication difficulties are experienced. Even if they are physically attractive, how will the audience understand them?

As a practical matter, Hollywood treats the deaf community as a linguistic minority; and as such, it has avoided substantive depictions of American Sign Language. At the individual level, Hollywood consistently has its deaf characters speak orally or simply lets the audience guess at the meaning of the deaf character's limited signs. The 1948 film *Johnny Belinda* used a hearing character, the doctor (played by Lew Ayres), to provide contextual clues to the signed dialogue with the deaf character (played by Jane Wyman), but at the time this was an exception to the general film practice. Another thirty-eight years passed before filmmakers again used this technique, in *Children of a*

Lesser God. Although this is not unlike the situation for Hispanic characters who must speak in accented English, it does explain why there are almost never two deaf characters in the same film. (The two notable exceptions are *The Heart Is a Lonely Hunter* and *Voices;* but in both films, when the two deaf characters communicate in signs, the audience is left to guess at the meaning of the dialogue.) Note that in *Children of a Lesser God,* when James (William Hurt) appears lost and isolated at the party of deaf people, the audience also has no idea what the deaf characters at the party are saying since he is not interpreting their signs.

The obvious solution to this dilemma is the use of captions, but the movie industry consistently has rejected their use since the transition from silent to talking motion pictures in the late twenties. In spite of occasional use of captions for foreign-language dialogue in such films as *The Longest Day* and *Patton,* theatrical films and television have opposed the use of open captions with the rationale that general audiences dislike them. This result has reduced the ability of scriptwriters to get beyond simple-minded dialogue for nonspeaking deaf characters and has perpetuated the practice of separate viewing for deaf audiences. In *Johnny Belinda* and *Children of a Lesser God,* the dialogue is complex, but the deaf person is wedded to a hearing person's voice, which reinforces the image of the deaf person as dependent.

This image has not been exclusively negative, however: *Johnny Belinda* did make a difference by demonstrating that deafness could be portrayed substantively and still turn a profit. After the film's success, there was a significant increase in the number of deaf characters in the movies and on television during the 1950s and following decades. Although many of the stereotypes continued unabated, there were films and television episodes that provided information to the general public about new developments in medicine, education, hearing-aid technology, and telecommunication devices. In 1968, *The Heart Is a Lonely Hunter* presented an English-literate nonspeaking deaf person, and finally, in 1979, the first professional deaf person, a teacher, appeared in *Voices.*

Unfortunately, the only three theatrical films produced in the first half of the eighties that deal with deafness appear to have returned to some of the old formulas. *Eyes of a Stranger* once again shows the cure of a deaf-blind-mute female victim through the device of a traumatic attack by a rapist. And although the screenwriters wrapped *Amy* in a historical guise, that story celebrates the triumph of articulation (lip-reading and speech) over dependence on sign language and a parochial deaf community. Finally, the most powerful and potentially independent deaf character to appear in motion pictures, Sarah, in *Children of a Lesser God,* is a cleaning woman who is dependent on a man who earns his living as a speech teacher.

In contrast, television has broken many of the prevalent stereotypes about deafness. A wide range of deaf adult characters have appeared as attorneys, illiterates, dancers, prostitutes, stuntwomen, and teachers; and they have been allowed to speak with clear voices or speech-impaired voices, or to remain mute. Although loneliness prevails in the continued predominance of melodramas, deaf couples have appeared in two television movies: *And Your Name Is Jonah* and *Love Is Never Silent.* The most significant and hopeful sign has been the appearance of deaf actors in the roles of deaf characters: since 1968 they have appeared with increasing frequency, capped by the December 1985 Hallmark Hall of Fame presentation of *Love Is Never Silent,* starring deaf actors Phyllis Frelich and Ed Waterstreet and produced by Julianna Fjeld, who is also deaf.

Even though many of the earlier and more pejorative filmic views of deafness will continue to appear on late-night television and on videotape recorders (through rentals), there has been a discernible change in the direction of the depiction of deafness in the eighties, led by television programming.[3] Since much of television continues to be produced in Hollywood, we can only hope that theatrical films will reflect these positive changes within the near future.

Some credit for this recent change in direction for television must be attributed to the presence of deaf persons as actors, technical advisers, and, most recently, as producers. Although most filmmakers would not accept the analogy of white actors in blackface, many in the deaf community perceive the continued use of hearing actors in the role of deaf characters as a present-day example of that silent era practice. When Daniel Wilson, the producer of the television program "Mom and Dad Can't Hear Me," responded to charges of discrimination by deaf actress Audree Norton, he argued that filmmakers should not limit deaf roles to deaf actors. Even though the facts are that less than 10 percent of the deaf character roles have been played by deaf actors and that virtually all of these have been on television, his argument struck a familiar and responsive chord in Hollywood. While the evidence makes his argument shallow, his rhetoric reflects a basic principle: actors should be free to play any role. Certainly, the testimony of the actors is clear.

Anthony Quinn, referring to his role as Deaf Smith, observed (or at least his publicist did) that "if every actor could play a deaf-mute once, it would be the best thing that could happen to him. I had to react to everything and everyone around me. It was a terrific experience for an actor."[4] Alan Arkin recognized that deaf people are as "multicolored and varied emotionally as they can be," but the "one thing that the affliction does seem to cause is a great sense of isolation."[5] In an effort to replicate the experience, Arkin watched television without sound and learned that a deaf lip-reader watches the face, not the lips.[6] Jane Wyman worked hard to capture the look of deafness, stuffing her ears with wax and arranging for a young deaf woman to visit her regularly. She strove for a look that tried to anticipate and guess at the meaning of the spoken word.[7]

All of this, of course, misses the point, because these excellent actors focused on the absence of hearing, not on deafness. Although there are actors who are oriented to a visual mode of communication, there have been few of them since the silent era. To use recent examples, the deaf actresses Phyllis Frelich and Marlee Matlin have few peers, among their hearing colleagues, in the use of facial expression and body language, not to mention sign language itself. Their portrayals of the charming deaf prostitute on "Barney Miller," the deaf mother of a hearing daughter in the television movie *Love Is Never Silent,* and Sarah in *Children of a Lesser God* exemplify the best of a long tradition of deaf actors and expose the shallowness of weak imitations by hearing actors.

Perhaps the silent film actor Lon Chaney understood this better than anyone else. Even with the high-tech gadgetry of modern filmmaking, few actors have been able to surpass Chaney's ability to master the look of a character. Although he was gifted at make-up artistry, he understood that characterization was more than cosmetics. This son of deaf parents understood, instinctively and experientially, what it meant to be different as well as to look different. Accordingly, he created memorable characterizations that remain classics today. So far, Hollywood has had limited success with the look of deafness.

Although some of the films discussed in this survey demonstrate insights into individual aspects of deafness, none of them deal with deafness in a way that reflects a cultural understanding of deaf people. Until filmmakers portray the existence of an active and healthy deaf community, it is improbable that Americans will get beyond the pathological myths that make daily life difficult for deaf individuals. In this sense, films continue to serve as a major source of public misinformation about deafness and deaf people. The deaf community awaits the next step in the industry's portrayal of deafness.

Earlier, I observed that the deaf community has a right to complain about its treatment by filmmakers; at the same time, I have been puzzled by the comparative absence of complaints. A few petitions in 1929 and a boycott fifty years later, in 1979, hardly represents significant protest. Much of this, I believe, can be attributed to our national policy of segregated film and television viewing for deaf audiences. Deafness is a disability of communication. And it is my opinion that the deaf community literally does not appreciate how badly they have fared at the hands of the entertainment industry. For most of the period covered by this survey of film and television, deaf viewers have not been given precise information about the dialogues that accompany the images on the screen. For example, within the past several months, *Beau Bandit* (1930), *Charlie Chan at the Olympics* (1936), *No Road Back* (1957), and *For the First Time* (1959) have appeared on television stations in the Washington, D.C., area. Despite the presence of what is considered to be the best-educated deaf community, Washington deaf audiences had no information about the audio content of these films because, like most past and current films, they were not captioned.

Even though most current prime-time network television programs are captioned for use with television decoders, the overwhelming majority of the films and episodes described in this survey, and in the Filmography, are not captioned. And, as exemplified by the appearance of old films in the Washington, D.C., television market, this backlog of films and episode reruns will continue to haunt the deaf community through the depiction of misinformation about deaf people. Simple equity requires that the industry, or the federal government, if need be, correct this communication imbalance with the provision of captioned versions so that the deaf community is fully informed. A society committed to a policy of equal access for all of its citizens can do no less.

NOTES

1. Molly Haskell, *From Reverence to Rape: The Treatment of Women in Movies* (New York: Penguin Books, 1974), pp. 1–41.

2. The three are: *Pocketful of Miracles* (United Artists, 1961), "Good Times" (CBS, 1975), and "Barney Miller" (ABC, 1981).

3. Although I do not agree that this has occurred with commercial films about deafness, this positive change has been observed for other disabilities. See Paul K. Longmore, "'Mask': A Revealing Portrayal of the Disabled," *Los Angeles Times Sunday Calendar* (May 5, 1985), pp. 22–23; and Longmore, "Screening Stereotypes: Images of Disabled People," *Social Policy* (Summer 1985), pp. 36-37.

4. *"Deaf Smith and Johnny Ears:* MGM Pressbook," C–37, Motion Picture, Broadcasting, and Recorded Sound Division, Library of Congress.

5. Alan Arkin to Virginia S. Carr, Personal Correspondence, September 22, 1970, Manuscript Department, Duke University, Durham, N.C.

6. Robert E. Miller, Transcript: American Film Institute Screenwriting Workshop, March 22, 1977 (Beverly Hills, Calif.: Center for Advanced Film Studies, 1977), pp. 26–27.

7. Joe Morella and Edward Epstein, *Jane Wyman, a Biography* (New York: Delacorte Press, 1985), p. 115.

Filmography

In 1986 the American Foundation for the Blind published *Images of Blind and Visually Impaired People in the Movies, 1913–1985, an Annotated Filmography with Notes*, the first substantive filmography to deal with a disabled population. No comparable list exists for deafness or deaf characters. This filmography represents a first effort to compile such a list of entertainment films, designed for general audiences, that deal with deafness or that include a deaf character in a major or pivotal role. Although I have identified nearly two hundred film or television citations (some of which are not included here for lack of verification), the information is sometimes sketchy; readers are invited to contact me with information about missing or additional films or television programs. Finally, some readers may object to the inclusion of certain films as unrelated to deafness; however, I have included such films when standard references have previously misidentified a deaf character.

This filmography has been compiled by consulting standard film references, motion picture industry trade newspapers, and copyright registration files at the Library of Congress. Often overlooked, copyright registrations are an inconsistent but frequently good source of information about early films and pre-videotape television programs. Although not all producers seek copyright protection, most do. For many of the early nitrate-based films, the registrations are sometimes the only source of information. Microfilm and manuscript copies of the registrations include information that varies in length from a one-page synopsis to complete scripts. These references have been supplemented with information from the nonpublished shelf listings of the media collections and the nonpublished vertical files of the deafness collections at the Gallaudet University Library, Washington, D.C. Most important have been references found in publications from the deaf community.

Although most deaf community publications are not indexed, they are a fruitful source of information about movies and television programs. For the silent film era, *The Silent Worker*, the *Deaf-Mutes' Journal*, the *Volta Review*, the *California News*, and the *Jewish Deaf News* are invaluable, as are the *Cavalier*, the *Deaf American (Silent Worker)*, and *The Frat* for the talkies and television. All of these publications can be found at the Gallaudet University Archives.

Individual films are scattered among film centers around the country, but a surprising number of the films are at the Motion Picture, Broadcasting, and Recorded Sound Division of the Library of Congress. The legislative history of the current copyright law makes it clear that Congress intended that non-profit institutions of higher education that serve deaf populations be able to copy off the air television broadcasts for captioning or redistribution to the deaf community. Accordingly, Gallaudet University has an excellent collection of recent television programs, and its nonpublished shelf lists and media catalog should be consulted for available films or television programs.

The films have been divided into two categories: motion pictures produced for general theatrical viewing; and television programs (note that commercial films subsequently rebroadcast on television are listed in the first category even though the television audience may have been larger). In addition, there is a final section of non-Hollywood sign-language motion pictures produced for the deaf community. Within these three categories, citations are listed chronologically. An asterisk preceding the synopsis indicates that I have actually viewed the film or television program described in the citation; if no film archive is listed, I saw the film on television or at a movie theater.

Movies and Deafness

1. *Deaf Mute Girl Reciting "Star Spangled Banner"* (American Muto-scope and Biograph, 1902), 1 reel, b&w, silent. Deaf character: unknown.
Synopsis: *As implied by the title, this is simply a performance of the national anthem. The woman who signs the national anthem uses American Sign Language (ASL).
Source: Since this film preceded the practice of copyright registration of actual film footage, it has been reconstructed from the paper print collection at the Library of Congress (hereafter, LC).

2. *Martyrs of the Alamo* (aka *Birth of Texas*) (Fine Arts, 1915), 5 reels, b&w, silent. Deaf character: Sam De Grasse.
Synopsis: *Based on the real Deaf Smith, who served as a scout for Sam Houston, the character in this film feigns deafness. In the first four reels, Silent Smith (De Grasse) is simply quiet when near the Mexicans. After the Alamo is lost, General Houston sends Smith to pose as a deaf-mute game hunter for Mexican General Santa Anna. Under suspicion, he signs "deaf" and passes a test of his hearing which allows him to then rescue his sweet-heart and return to General Houston for the battle that secures Texas's independence from Mexico.
Source: Film Collection, LC.

3. *The Silent Voice* (Quality Pictures, 1915), b&w, silent. Deaf character: Francis X. Bushman.

Synopsis: Bushman plays musician Franklyn Starr, who loses his hearing and his mother and "becomes a misanthrope, gloomy, and despondent." He retreats to the country where, unable to hear a warning, he is injured in a dynamite blast. He is nursed back to health by Marjorie Blair (Marguerite Snow), and their subsequent marriage survives his mistrust. He eventually recovers his hearing.

Source: Copyright Registration, LP 6445. No film has been found. (Hereafter, the latter is included to indicate that I have not found the film but continue to seek its location.)

4. *Menace of the Mute* (Pathes Freres, 1916), silent. Deaf character: unknown.

Synopsis: From the Ashton Kirk, Investigator, series. The murderer is mute. Kirk finds one of the notes the mute has written to a friend that identifies the mute as the murderer.

Source: Copyright Registration, LU 6920. No film has been found.

5. *The Dumb Bandit* (Rex, 1916), b&w, silent. Producer: Francis Ford. Script by Grace Cunard. Deaf character: Francis Ford.

Synopsis: Ford is a sheepherder who dons a mask and reappears as a "dumb" bandit to test the loyalty of his wife. In the climax, he pulls a gun and tells her "in dumb he is going to kill her husband." She pleads with him and they scuffle; when his mask falls off she sees that he is really her sheepherder husband. She repents and he promises not to leave her alone so long.

Source: *Moving Picture World* (March 9, 1916), 1700. No film has been found.

6. *The Dummy* (Paramount/Artcraft, 1917), b&w, silent. Deaf character: Jack Pickford.

Synopsis: This is a film version of a popular stage play in which a married couple agree to separate but cannot decide who should get custody of their daughter. When she is kidnapped, the detective agency hired to find the little girl employs a young man (Pickford) to masquerade as a "wealthy deaf and dumb boy," as bait for the kidnappers. Pickford eventually rescues the girl.

Source: Copyright Registration, LP 10289; *Variety Film Review* (March 17, 1917), p. 25. No film has been found.

7. *Deliverance* (Helen Keller Films, 1919), 7 reels, b&w, silent. Deaf characters: Etna Ross and Ann Mason play Keller as a young girl and maiden, respectively. Keller appears as herself in womanhood.

Synopsis: *Subtitled "The Most Wonderful Woman in the World, Helen Keller," this film was a product of Keller's ongoing search for financial support. Although it received positive reviews, it was not a financial success, and Keller thereafter devoted her energy to raising funds for the American

Foundation for the Blind, which in turn supported her financially. The film contrasts the lives of Keller and her girlhood friend, Nadja. Keller, who is "blind-deaf-and dumb!" graduates from college and becomes a world-known personality; Nadja, with all her faculties, lives a life of poverty and tragedy. Although finger spelling into the hand is depicted, the film emphasizes the importance of speech. The final caption reads: "Only those are blind who do not see the truth. Only those are deaf who do not hear the oracle of their better selves."

Source: George Kleine Film Collection, LC.

8. *The Miracle Man* (Paramount/Artcraft, 1919), b&w, silent. Producer: Mayflower. Director: George L. Tucker. Screenplay by George L. Tucker, based on a play by George M. Cohan and a short story by Frank L. Packard. Deaf character: Joseph J. Dowling.

Synopsis: A gang of fakes uses a deaf-blind man to "heal" them and thereby dupe hopefuls into giving them money for cures. Lon Chaney plays a fake cripple, Frog, who is regularly cured by the deaf-blind faith healer. When a young boy is actually cured, the gang is inspired to mend their individual lives and give up their crooked ways.

Sources: Copyright Registration, LP 14072; *New York Times Film Review* (August 27, 1919), 9:5; *Variety Film Review* (August 29, 1919), p. 66.

9. *Bits of Life* (Marshall Neilan, 1921), b&w, silent. Deaf character: unknown.

Synopsis: This film contains four short stories held together by the theme of the good samaritan's deeds gone wrong. One episode, "The Man Who Heard Everything," depicts the life of a deaf barber, who receives a hearing-aid device from a good samaritan, whereupon he discovers that his friends are corrupt and his wife is unfaithful. He subsequently destroys the device and becomes deaf again. Because of the presence of Lon Chaney in one of the episodes and the fact that Chaney's own deaf father was a barber, this film is one of the few pieces of circumstantial evidence of a deaf community perspective on the part of the famous character actor.

Sources: Copyright Registration, LP 17129; *Variety Film Review* (October 21, 1921), p. 35; Photo Stills, George Eastman House. No film has been found, but the photographs include one of the "deaf" barber, as yet unidentified.

10. *A Voice in the Dark* (Goldwyn, 1921), 5 reels, b&w, silent. Story by Ralph E. Dyar. Scenario by Frank Lloyd and Arthur Statter. Deaf character: Gertrude Norman.

Synopsis: *A deaf witness to a murder accuses a young woman on the basis of what she saw; a blind witness correctly identifies the guilty party on the basis of an overheard conversation, and thereby frees the young woman mistakenly identified by the deaf witness. The film's setting is a sanatorium where the two witnesses are patients. Norman's screen credit reads: "Mrs. Maria Lyiard. Deaf, and with an irritable disposition" and Alec Francis is "Joseph Crampton. Sightless, but still loving life and nature." The deaf character lip-reads with the assistance of an "aurophone."

Sources: One reel of five at LC; Manuscripts, MGM Collection, University of Southern California Performing Arts Archives (hereafter, USC); Photo Stills, Wisconsin Center for Film and Theatre Research (hereafter, Wisc.).

11. *The Man Who Played God* (United Artists, 1922), b&w, silent. Based on a story by Gouverneur Morris and a play, *The Silent Voice,* by Jules Eckert Goodman. Deaf character: George Arliss.

Synopsis: This film appeared in four versions: (1) 1915, as *Silent Voice;* (2) 1922, silent; (3) 1932, talking picture; and (4) 1955, retitled *Sincerely Yours.* Although the silent versions have not been found, a reading of the scripts and copyright registrations reveals that they differed little in substance from the 1932 talking version. George Arliss, the main character in both versions, plays a concert pianist who loses his hearing as a result of a bomb explosion. He retreats from his friends and the public to his penthouse apartment overlooking Central Park. Foiled in his attempt to commit suicide, he learns to lip-read and with the use of binoculars is soon lip-reading the stories of people in the park. Through his philanthropy he helps the park people solve their problems, which restores his faith in God. In the end he falls and regains his hearing (this was the same ending as the stage play; in the sound remake, he remains deaf). In all versions the speed by which he learns to lip-read is phenomenal. In the 1922 and 1932 versions there is a discussion of heredity and deafness.

Sources: *Man Who Played God* (Warner, 1932), United Artists Collection, Wisc.; Manuscripts, Wisc.; Warner Bros. Manuscript Collection, USC; George Arliss, *My Ten Years in the Studios* (Boston: Little, Brown, 1940).

12. *The Hunchback of Notre Dame* (Universal Jewel, 1923), 12 reels, b&w, silent. Director: Wallace Warsley. Deaf characters: Lon Chaney, John Cossar.

Synopsis: *This is the classic story of Quasimodo (Chaney), who comes to the rescue of a gypsy woman. It sometimes is forgotten that the hunchback Quasimodo is deafened because of his job as bellringer at the Cathedral of Notre Dame and as a result cannot understand the questions of an equally deafened judge (Cossar), who sentences Quasimodo to a public whipping.

Source: Museum of Modern Art, New York (hereafter, MOMA). There have been several remakes of this film.

13. *The Silent Stranger* (R-C Pictures, 1924), b&w, silent. Director: Albert Rogell. Story by Stewart Heisler. Deaf character: Fred Thompson.

Synopsis: A secret service agent named Jack Taylor, disguised as a deaf-mute, investigates a series of thefts of the U.S. mail. Aided by his horse, Silver

King, Taylor captures the gang of thieves and marries the postmaster's daughter.

Source: Copyright Registration, LP 20066. No film has been found.

14. *Siege* (Universal, 1925), 7 reels, b&w, silent. Deaf character: Marc MacDermott.

Synopsis: Augusta Ruyland (Mary Alden) runs the town where she owns a factory. Unwilling to accept her new, modern daughter-in-law, she dominates the family. The "pathetic mute" nephew likes the daughter-in-law and sends her flowers, but he commits suicide after his family finds out and ridicules him. Because he has willed his shares in the company to the younger woman, Ruyland loses control of the company and contemplates suicide, but she is saved by the daughter-in-law.

Source: *Motion Picture News* (1925), 3075.

15. *His Busy Hour* (independently produced by James Spearing and Bertha Lincoln Heustis, 1926), b&w, silent. All-deaf cast, including Albert Ballin (others unknown).

Synopsis: There is no evidence that this film was ever distributed commercially. James Spearing was a former *New York Times* film reviewer and Paramount scriptwriter. Deaf publications report a New York City showing to a deaf audience in order to solicit funds for distribution.

Source: *New York Times* (Dec. 12, 1926), VIII, 7:1. No film has been found.

16. *You'd Be Surprised* (Paramount, 1926), 6 reels, b&w, silent. Director: Arthur Rosson. Script by Jules Furthman. Captions by Robert Benchley and Ralph Spence. Deaf character: Granville Redmond.

Synopsis: *Raymond Griffith stars as the coroner-sleuth in this comedy–murder mystery. Integral to the plot is the presence of a deaf valet, who witnessed the murder; in a surprise ending, the deaf valet turns out to be a hearing deputy coroner who feigned deafness. However, the bigger surprise is that the deaf valet is played by a real deaf actor, Granville Redmond. Finger spelling, some signs, and nearly every visual stereotype of deafness are displayed in this film, even though Redmond's deafness was unknown to contemporary audiences and film reviewers.

Source: American Film Institute (AFI)/Paramount Collection, LC.

17. *An Italian Straw Hat* (Albatross/Sequana, 1927), 3 reels, b&w, silent. Director: Rene Clair. Screenplay by Rene Clair based on a stage play, *Un Chapeau de Paille D'Italie,* by Eugene Labiche and Marc Michel. Deaf character: Paul Olivier.

Synopsis: *On the way to the wedding, the bridegroom's horse eats a lady's hat. The lady's lover demands a replacement, and the result is a series of mishaps and visual gags, one of which revolves about a deaf man, Uncle Vezinet (Olivier) . He is oblivious to noise and the general chaos around him; further humor results when his ear trumpet is stuffed with paper. There is no sign language, and the film includes standard stereotypes of hard-of-hearing persons as objects of humor.

Source: Film Collection, MOMA.

18. *The Ridin Rowdy* (Pathe Exchange, 1927), b&w, silent.

Synopsis: This is another film in which a hearing character feigns deafness.

Source: AFI Index, F2.4599. No film has been found.

19. *The Flying Marine* (Columbia, 1929), b&w, sound. Deaf character: Ben Lyon.

Synopsis: Injured performing movie stunts, a former marine pilot (Lyon) loses his hearing. His brother (Jason Robards) and their mutual girlfriend raise money for an operation to restore the pilot's hearing. When his hearing returns, he learns of his girlfriend's love for his brother. Lyon continues his stunt flying, which results in his death, but only after he saves his brother's life.

Source: *Motion Picture News* (November 2, 1929), p. 94. No film has been found.

20. *The Dummy* (Paramount/Famous Players Lasky, 1929), b&w, sound. Deaf character: Mickey Bennett.

Synopsis: See film no. 6. Ruth Chatterton and Frederick March star as the parents of the kidnapped daughter; Bennett plays the young detective who feigns deafness to infiltrate the gang of kidnappers.

Sources: *Variety Film Review* (March 6, 1929), p. 21; *New York Times Film Review* (March 4, 1929), p. 2. No film has been found.

21. *Beau Bandit* (RKO, 1930), 2 reels, b&w, sound. Deaf character: Mitchell Lewis.

Synopsis: *Rod LaRoque plays a Hispanic bandit who has a reputation as a killer but turns out to be the hero in this western. His sidekick is the deaf-mute Colosso. LaRoque uses a few primitive signs and gestures, and Colosso survives by lip-reading his adversaries and feeling the vibration of approaching posses.

Source: United Artists Collection, Wisc.

22. *Mountain Justice* (Universal, 1930) b&w, sound. Deaf character: Ken Maynard.

Synopsis: Maynard plays a cowboy whose father is shot after receiving a warning note. He feigns deafness to force individuals to communicate through notes, thereby allowing him to compare each suspect's handwriting with that of the warning note. Maynard succeeds in finding the culprit and marries the leading lady. This film should not be confused with a 1937 film of the same title.

Source: Copyright Registration, LP 1232. No film has been found.

23. *Sarah and Son* (Paramount/Famous Players Lasky, 1930), b&w, sound. Deaf character: unknown.

Synopsis: Ruth Chatterton and Fredric March star in this story of a mother who is forced to give up her child. Years later when she tries to regain custody, the new parents attempt to trick her by substituting a deaf child, but they do not succeed.

Source: Copyright Registration, LP 1169. No film has been found.

24. *The Man Who Played God* (Warner, 1932), 2 reels, b&w, sound. Director: John Adolphi. Based on a story by Gouverneur Morris and a stage play by Jules E. Goodman. Deaf character: George Arliss.

Synopsis: *See film no. 11. In this version, Royal, the concert pianist, remains deaf. Also, the film features an incredible lip-reading test wherein the lip-reading teacher (a real deaf educator recruited from a New York school for deaf children) places his fist in front of his mouth when speaking and Royal still understands him perfectly, "partially from the lips and the muscles of the jaw."

Source: See film no. 11.

25. *Charlie Chan at the Olympics* (Twentieth Century–Fox, 1936), b&w, sound. Producer: John Stone. Director: H. Bruce Humberstone. Screenplay by Robert Ellis and Helen Logan, based on an original story by Paul Burger. Deaf character: unknown.

Synopsis: *A secret radio-aeroguidance device is stolen and Charlie Chan (Warner Oland) tracks it down in Berlin, the site of the Olympic Games. Foreign spies and industrial competitors try to take it away from Chan. One of the competitors hires a deaf man to lip-read a conversation between Chan and one of the foreign spies, using high-powered binoculars. Signs and finger spelling are used correctly in this sequence.

Source: Scripts, Theater Arts Library, University of California, Los Angeles (hereafter, UCLA).

26. *Sins of Man* (Twentieth Century–Fox, 1936), b&w, sound. Producer: Kenneth Macgowan. Directors: Gregory Ratoff and Otto Brower. Script based on novel *Job* by Joseph Roth. Deaf character: Mickey Rentschler.

Synopsis: Jean Hersholt stars as an Austrian bellringer. His wife dies in childbirth and Hersholt seeks help for the child, who is deaf. They are separated and Hersholt becomes a derelict. The child's hearing is restored in a World War I accident and he eventually becomes a famous orchestra conducter. When Hersholt hears the orchestra play a familiar Austrian melody, he is reunited with his lost son.

Source: Jay R. Nash and Stanley R. Ross, *The Motion Picture Guide* (Chicago: Cinebooks, 1987), vol. 7, p. 2944. No film has been found.

27. *The Story of Alexander Graham Bell* (Twentieth Century–Fox, 1939), 10 reels, b&w, sound. Producer: Darryl F. Zanuck. Director: Irving Cummings. Screenplay by Lamar Trotti, based on a story by Ray Harris. Deaf characters: Bobs Watson and Loretta Young.

Synopsis: *This is primarily the story of Bell's invention of the telephone and the subsequent legal battle to protect his patent. The first reel deals with Bell as a teacher of the deaf, and there are excellent scenes of his pupil, George Sanders (Watson), and their famous (in the annals of deaf education) alphabet glove. Young stars as Mabel Hubbard, an oral deaf woman who lip-reads perfectly and speaks clearly. Hubbard marries Bell (Don Ameche) and encourages his experiments with the telephone.

Source: First reel, LC; Gallaudet University Media Collection (hereafter, GU Media); Scripts, Theater Arts Library, UCLA; Copyright Registration, LP 8838. Although the Library of Congress only possesses the first reel of this film, the copyright registration includes the complete script, reel by reel.

28. *And Now Tomorrow* (Paramount, 1944), sound. Executive Producer: B. G. DeSylva. Director: Irving Pichel. Screenplay by Frank Partos and Raymond Chandler, based on a novel by Rachel Field. Deaf character: Loretta Young.

Synopsis: Young stars as a beautiful, rich, deaf woman who communicates via unaccented speech and lip-reading. Alan Ladd plays a young man from the wrong side of the tracks who becomes a doctor in the town dominated by Young's factory-owner father. Young discovers that her fiancé (Barry Sullivan) prefers her younger sister (Susan Hayward), thanks to experimental drugs she receives from Ladd which eventually cure her deafness; she also discovers that she truly loves Ladd and goes to him. The movie features an emergency mastoid operation performed by Ladd, who is assisted by Young.

Source: Copyright Registration, LP 12962.

29. *Out of the Past* (RKO, 1947), 3 reels, b&w, sound. Deaf character: Dickie Moore.

Synopsis: *A gangster (Kirk Douglas) confronts a gas station owner (Robert Mitchum) with unfinished business from Mitchum's past life as a detective. A "deaf kid" works for Mitchum and they communicate via signs and finger spelling, which are generally unintelligible. The deaf kid saves Mitchum's life through a remarkable cast with his fishing rod.

Source: United Artists Collection, Wisc.

30. *Johnny Belinda* (Warner, 1948), 3 reels, b&w, sound. Producer: Jerry Wald. Director: Jean Negulesco. Screenplay by Irmgard Von Cube and Allen Vincent, based on a stage play by Elmer Harris. Deaf character: Jane Wyman.

Synopsis: *This is the story of an illiterate deaf woman, known locally as the "dummy," who lives on a rundown farm in Nova Scotia with her father (Charles Bickford) and aunt (Agnes Moorehead). A sympathetic physician (Lew Ayres) takes an interest in her and teaches her signs and finger spelling, through which she is transformed into an intelligent, communicative, and attractive young woman. A local bully (Steve McNally, who played the doctor on the Broadway stage) rapes her and she later gives birth to a son,

Johnny. The bully and his new bride (Jan Sterling) fight to adopt the child, arguing that a deaf person is an unfit mother. Wyman shoots McNally when he tries to take the baby away and is tried for murder. In the dramatic climax, the wife confesses that her husband raped Wyman, who regains Johnny and goes off to marry the doctor. Wyman remains mute throughout the film, and although some scenes are far-fetched (such as her noiseless delivery of the baby), we see a sympathetic portrayal of deafness and sign language. Even though the film is not captioned, most deaf viewers can understand the story; and hearing audiences can understand Wyman because other characters voice her lines or respond in a way that makes her signed speech clear.

Source: United Artists Collection, Wisc.; Press Kits, LC; Manuscripts, Warner Bros. Collection, USC.

31. *Moonrise* (Republic, 1948), 90 min., b&w, sound. Producer: Charles Haas. Director: Frank Borzage. Screenplay by Charles Hass, based on a novel of the same title by Theodore Strauss. Deaf character: Harry Morgan.

Synopsis: Danny Hawkins (Dane Clark) is taunted throughout his childhood because his father was executed as a murderer. When Danny accidentally kills one of the town bullies, he is distraught to find the murder weapon in the hands of a deaf-mute named Billy Scripture (Morgan). He nearly kills Scripture but later repents and confesses his crime.

Source: Copyright Registration, LP 1852; Script, USC. Although not available for viewing, UCLA has a print.

32. *No Way Out* (Twentieth Century–Fox, 1950), 9 reels, b&w, sound. Producer: Darryl F. Zanuck. Director: Joseph L. Mankiewicz. Screenplay by Joseph L. Mankiewicz and Lesser Samuels. Deaf character: Harry Bellaver.

Synopsis: *Sidney Poitier plays a black doctor who treats two armed robbers the police have wounded and captured. One of the robbers dies during treatment and the surviving robber-brother, a vicious racist (Richard Widmark), accuses the doctor of intentionally killing his brother. Another brother is a deaf-mute (Bellaver) who reads comic books and can lip-read; the two brothers and the deceased brother's wife (Linda Darnell) all use signs (generally accurately and in a sympathetic manner). The only way Poitier can prove his innocence is through an autopsy, which the family refuses; eventually, however, he is cleared.

Source: Film Collection, LC; Manuscripts, Twentieth Century–Fox Collections, USC.

33. *Crash of Silence* (aka *Mandy*) (Ealing Studios, 1952), 11 reels, b&w, sound. Producer: Leslie Norman. Director: Alexander MacKendrick. Screenplay by Nigel Balchin and Jack Whittingham, based on the novel *The Day Is Ours* by Hilda Lewis. Deaf character: Mandy Miller.

Synopsis: *This English drama portrays a family's effort to cope with their deaf child. Initially, the family isolates the child (played by a hearing child, Mandy Miller) and keeps her at home in London until she is nearly six years old. After a brush with death, when Mandy fails to hear an approaching automobile, her mother (Phyllis Calvert) takes her to a residential school (which is, in fact, the Royal Residential School for the Deaf in Manchester), where they meet the superintendent (Jack Hawkins), who provides an opportunity for a documentary-like explanation of speech and lip-reading pedagogy. Mandy does not do well at the school until the superintendent arranges for special tutoring and day attendance; the father (Terrance Morgan) suspects that the superintendent is more interested in the mother than in Mandy. The climax of the film has Mandy finally talking.

Source: Film Collection, LC.

34. *The Big Sky* (Winchester; rel., RKO, 1952), 16 reels, b&w, sound. Producer and director: Howard Hawks. Deaf character: none.

Synopsis: *This western is one of several films that feature Indians who communicate in the sign language of the Plains Indians. Elizabeth Threatt is featured as a Blackfoot Indian princess who does not speak English but occasionally uses signs.

Source: Film Collection, LC.

35. *Walk East on Beacon* (RD-DR Productions; rel., Columbia, 1952), 11 reels, b&w, sound. Producer: Louis de Rochemont. Deaf character: none.

Synopsis: *Lip-reading is featured in this quasi-documentary account of the capture of a spy ring by the FBI, which emphasizes the modern scientific and forensic methods of the Bureau. Students at the "Plummer School of Lip-reading" read the lips of foreign spies shown in an FBI surveillance film, reinforcing the stereotypes about lip-readers. Although it is clear in the film that the students can hear, deaf publications (e.g., *The Frat*) have identified the students as deaf.

Source: Film Collection, LC.

36. *All of Me* (Twentieth Century–Fox, 1953). Deaf character: Johnny Ray.

Synopsis: This is a biographical sketch of the popular hard-of-hearing singer Johnny Ray.

Source: "Spotlight," *The Frat* (March 1953). No film has been found.

37. *Flesh and Fury* (aka *Hear No Evil*) (Universal-International, 1952), 82 min., sound. Producer: Leonard Goldstein. Director: Joseph Pevney. Screenplay by Bernard Gordon. Deaf character: Tony Curtis.

Synopsis: This is the story of a deaf boxer, Dummy Callan (Curtis), who initially does not speak or use signs. A scheming, attractive female (Jan Sterling) manipulates herself into a position whereby she dominates his boxing career and pushes him into matches that his trainer feels are risky. Prior to a big fight, a magazine reporter (Mona Freeman), whose deceased father was deaf, arrives to interview Callan and signs to him. At first he refuses to respond, but she eventually gains his trust. Callan later undergoes an operation that restores his hearing (he also takes speech lessons), but he winds up losing his sense of timing as a boxer. Recognizing his ineffectiveness, Sterling bets against him. During the championship fight, Callan again loses his hearing; he regains his timing and wins, and afterward he admits that he was confused by and afraid of the new world of sound. As he leaves the arena with Freeman, it becomes apparent that his hearing loss from the fight was temporary. Source: Final Screenplay, Leonard Goldstein Collection, Academy of Motion Picture Arts and Sciences (hereafter, AMPAS).

38. *The Green Scarf* (B&A Productions, 1954), 12 reels, b&w, sound. Producer: Bertram Ostrer. Director: George M. O'Ferrall. Screenplay by Gordon Wellesley based on the novel *The Brute* by Guy Des Cars. Deaf character: Kieron Moore.

Synopsis: *This English film is set in France, where a deaf-blind man (Moore), who has written a successful autobiography, is accused of murder. Because he believes that his wife (Ann Todd) committed the murder, he refuses to communicate or cooperate in his defense. The attorney (Michael Redgrave) assigned to defend him proves the innocence of both the accused and his wife through a test of the deaf-blind man's sense of color—the green scarf. In flashbacks we learn of his early life and his education at a French Catholic school for the blind. Finger spelling into the hand is used in the film but is unintelligible.
Source: Film Collection, LC.

39. *The Story of Esther Costello* (Valiant/Columbia, 1955), 10 reels, b&w, sound. Producers: John and James Woolf. Director: David Miller. Based on Nicholas Monsarrat's novel *The Golden Virgin*. Deaf character: Heather Sears.

Synopsis: *This film depicts the story of a young woman (Sears) who becomes deaf and blind as the result of a bomb explosion in her Irish village, which also results in the death of her mother. She grows up under brutish conditions, until the local priest convinces a visiting rich American (Joan Crawford) to adopt her. Crawford enrolls Esther in a school in the United States, but when she leaves, Esther runs into the street, where she is nearly hit by an automobile. Crawford decides to remain at the school and learns how to teach Esther through finger spelling and Braille (although she progresses much too quickly, the lessons and finger spelling are clear). After giving an inspirational speech at a nearby school, the two women participate in efforts to raise money for deaf-blind children. At this juncture Crawford's wayward husband (Rossano Brazzi) returns and deceives his wife into cooperating with a worldwide crooked fundraising campaign. The husband rapes Esther, which so traumatizes her that her hearing, vision, and speech are restored. Esther ends the campaign and Crawford kills her husband and herself.

Source: Film Collection, LC.

40. *Sincerely Yours* (Warner/International Artists, 1955). 15 reels, color, sound. Based on a stage play by Jules Eckert Goodman. Deaf character: Liberace.

Synopsis: *This film is a remake of *The Man Who Played God* (see film nos. 11, 24) and includes many concert performance scenes by Liberace. In terms of deafness, the only difference is that the main character's hearing loss is the result of otosclerosis; thus, he regains his hearing in mid-picture only to lose it again. The film concludes with a successful fenestration operation, enabling the pianist to perform for his fans. Note that Liberace describes the binoculars he uses to read the lips of people in the park as the same powerful kind made by Germans for use by deaf-mutes in Turkey to lip-read foreign diplomats.

Source: Film Collection, LC.

41. *Shield for Murder* (United Artists, 1955), sound. Deaf character: David Myer.

Synopsis: A detective (Edmund O'Brien) kills a bookie and steals $25,000. An old deaf-mute (Myer) witnesses the killing and is murdered after he reports it to the police. A young detective (John Agar) tracks the killer.

Source: No film has been found.

42. *The Prodigal* (rel., MGM, 1955), 14 reels, color, sound. Director: Richard Thorpe. Deaf character: none.

Synopsis: *The prodigal son, Michah (Edmund Purdom), saves the runaway slave, Asham (Cameron Mitchell), a mute, who has been sentenced to death for stirring up a slave revolt. Deaf publications incorrectly reported the mute character as deaf, which was not an uncommon occurrence.

Source: Film Collection, LC.

43. *No Road Back* (RKO, 1956), b&w, sound. Producer: Steven Pallos. Director: Montgomery Tully. Screenplay by Charles A. Leeds and Montgomery Tully. Deaf character: Margaret Rawlings.

Synopsis: *A blind-deaf London nightclub owner (Rawlings) lets a gang use her club as the base of their criminal operations and she uses her share of the loot to support the medical studies of her son in America. The gang later frames her son for murder. She locks the leader in her office and, with the aid of her guide dog, shoots at him in an effort to force a confession. While she succeeds in saving her son, she is killed in the process. Although she speaks throughout the film, others communicate to her through her companion-interpreter, who finger spells the English manual alphabet into her hand.

Sources: Copyright Registration, PA 255–100; Film Collection, LC.

44. *Man of a Thousand Faces* (Columbia, 1957), 13 reels, b&w, sound.

Producer: Robert Author. Director: Joseph Pevney. Screenplay by R. Wright Campbell, Ivan Goff, and Ben Roberts, based on a story by Ralph Wheelwright. Deaf characters: Celia Lovsky and Nolan Leary.

Synopsis: *This biographical film of the silent film star Lon Chaney (James Cagney), whose parents (Lovsky and Leary) were deaf, provides good insights into a deaf family and outsiders' reactions to deafness. The film describes Chaney's childhood fights in response to taunts about his parents, his reluctance to tell his first wife (played by Dorothy Malone) about his parents' deafness, his parents' normal family life with four hearing children, and his wife's fear that their child would be born deaf. Although generally not voiced or translated for hearing audiences, the signs and finger spelling are clear; none of the dialogue is captioned for deaf audiences. Chaney's family is depicted as happy, with a normal life-style.

Source: Film Collection, LC.

45. *The Proud Rebel* (Formosa; rel., Buena Vista, 1958), 11 reels, color, sound. Producer: Samuel Goldwyn, Jr. Director: Michael Curtiz. Screenplay by Joseph Petracca and Lillie Hayward, based on a story by James E. Grant. Mute character who signs: David Ladd.

Synopsis: *Alan Ladd stars as a former Civil War rebel who seeks medical help for his son David, a mute, who uses signs and speaks in an impaired voice. After local children taunt David as a "dummy," the father sells their only asset, a champion sheepdog, to pay for an operation to restore David's speech. Initially unsuccessful, David later speaks his father's name and saves him from an ambush. There is no explanation of how or why David first learned signs, which Ladd interprets through appropriate responses. Although occasionally unclear, most of the sign communication is correct.

Source: Film Collection, LC.

46. *Maracaibo* (MGM, 1958), color, sound. Producer and director: Cornel Wilde. Script by Ted Sherdeman, based on a novel by Stirling Silliphant. Mute character who signs: Francis Lederer.

Synopsis: Cornel Wilde plays a firefighter hired to put out an offshore oil fire. The oil well owner is a mute (Lederer) who communicates via signs. His aide, played by Michael Landon, interprets for him.

Source: *Variety* (May 14, 1958). No film has been found.

47. *The Tingler* (Columbia, 1959), b&w, sound. Producer and director: William Castle. Written by Robb White. Deaf character: Judith Evelyn.

Synopsis: *The deaf-mute owner of a theater that shows silent movies communicates with her husband via finger spelling and a few assorted awkward signs. The husband explains to a pathologist (Vincent Price) that "she's deaf and dumb but she reads lips if you look straight at her. She can't make a sound and can't hear a sound." Price says that she has no vocal chords, an inaccurate piece of information about deafness that becomes the basis of the

plot. The diabolic pathologist "discovers" that unless human fear can be relieved by a scream, a parasitic organism is produced that can split the spinal chord, and he intentionally frightens the theater owner (Evelyn) in an attempt to capture the parasitic "tingler" organism that emerges from her back after she silently dies of fright. This horror film, when shown in theaters, used "percepto" (wired theater seats) to provide a "tingle" on cue.
Source: Videotape rental.

48. *For the First Time* (rel., MGM, 1959), 11 reels, color, sound. Director: Rudolph Mate. Original story and screenplay by Andrew Solt. Deaf character: Johanna von Koszian.
Synopsis: *Tony Costa (Mario Lanza) is an infamous opera singer. He falls in love with a young woman (von Koszian) who is deaf but lip-reads and speaks perfectly; she refuses to marry him unless she can hear. While on a concert tour they visit ear specialists, who refuse to treat her using the new but dangerous experimental surgery techniques. She finally convinces one doctor to operate, and she wakes up after surgery to Costa singing the "Ave Maria." Later, she contracts a virus and loses her hearing again; Costa blames himself, but she eventually recovers.
Source: Film Collection, LC.

49. *The Adventures of Huckleberry Finn* (MGM, 1960), 6 reels, color, sound. Producer: Samuel Goldwyn, Jr. Director: Michael Curtiz. Script by James Lee, based on a novel by Mark Twain. Deaf character: unknown.
Synopsis: *In one episode two river con artists, the King (Tony Randall) and the Duke of Bilgewater (Mickey Shaughnessy), pretend to be an English minister accompanied by his deaf brother, the Duke, and a young nephew, Huck (Eddie Hodges). The Duke parodies signs in order to abscond with a dead man's gold. When the real English cousins of the dead man arrive, they communicate in correct signs, whereupon Huck escapes to the river and the King and Duke are taken to jail. In an earlier episode, the slave Jim (Archie Moore) confesses to Huck that he is a sinner because he once hit his daughter for failing to obey him. Learning that his daughter failed to respond because she was deaf from scarlet fever, Jim feels guilty about his behavior.
Source: Film Collection, LC. See also Henry Nash Smith, ed., *Adventures of Huckleberry Finn by Mark Twain* (Cambridge, Mass.: Riverside Press, 1958), pp. 132–72.

50. *Happiness of Us Alone* (*Namonaku Mazushiku Utsukushiku*) (Toho Co., 1961), sound. Producers: Sanezumi Fujimotu and Kenjiro Tsunoda. Directed and screenplay by Zenzo Matsuyama. Deaf characters: Hideko Takamine and Keiju Kobayashi.
Synopsis: Takamine and Kobayashi play a deaf couple who use Japanese signs. Although their first child dies as a result of their inability to hear, the film is sympathetic in its depiction of the couple's growth as a "loving, self-

respecting" family. The distributors of this Japanese film, which carries English subtitles, advertised it as "in the Johnny Belinda" tradition.

Sources: Press Kits, AMPAS; AFI Index, F6.2040. No film has been found.

51. *Mumu* (Mosfilm, 1961), sound. Producers and directors: Anotoli Bobrowsky and Yeugeni Teterin. Adapted from a story by Ivan Turgenev. Deaf character: Afanasi Kochetkov.

Synopsis: This film, about loneliness and the need for love, features a huge deaf-mute field hand who is brought to Moscow to work. He dislikes the city and is lonely, until he finds a sick puppy to nurse back to health. He names the dog "Mumu," the only word he can articulate. When the dog offends his mistress, she orders him to kill it. He does, then walks away from the estate.

Sources: AFI Index, F6.3333; *New York Times Film Review* (June 5, 1961), 37:4.

52. *Pocketful of Miracles* (United Artists, 1961), 15 reels, color, sound. Producer and director: Frank Capra. Based on a Damon Runyon story. Deaf character: Ellen Corby.

Synopsis: *The film depicts a band of Broadway peddlers, a cripple, a dwarf, a blind man, and a deaf flower peddler (Corby), who pay Apple Annie (Bette Davis) a monthly fee to work the street. Annie uses the money to support a daughter in Europe, who believes that her mother is actually wealthy and of high social standing. When the daughter brings her fiancé to New York to meet her mother, Annie is transformed, with the help of her friends and a special patron, into a beautiful lady who lives in a New York City penthouse. The deaf flower peddler uses authentic sign language but must read lips throughout the film since no one else signs to her, even though all of her peddler friends and Annie understand and translate her signs. Capra made an earlier version of this film, *Lady for a Day* (Columbia, 1933); standard references identify the panhandler characters as the "blind man" and "shorty."

Source: Film Collection, LC.

53. *The Miracle Worker* (United Artists, 1962), 12 reels, b&w, sound. Producer: Fred Coe. Director: Arthur Penn. Screenplay by William Gibson, based on his play adapted from *The Story of My Life* by Helen Keller. Deaf character: Patty Duke.

Synopsis: *Anne Sullivan's pedagogy consists of continuous finger spelling into Helen Keller's hand until the young deaf-blind girl achieves understanding of the link between finger spelling and words (concepts). The symbol of this understanding, and the climax of the film, is depicted in the utterance "wah-wah" (water). The finger spelling is clear and accurate throughout the film, but for individuals familiar with American Sign Language, it is disconcerting to see that Keller's gesture for her mother is the standard sign for "prostitute"; however, since this same sign-gesture appears in the 1919 silent film *Deliverance,* and presumably was approved by both Helen Keller and

Anne Sullivan Macy, one must assume that it is authentic.
Source: Film Collection, LC.

54. *Lassie's Great Adventure* (Wrather Corp.; rel., Twentieth Century–Fox, 1963), sound. Deaf character: Richard Kiel.
Synopsis: Lassie and his young master are carried away in a hot-air balloon to Canada, where they are lost. A deaf-mute Indian, Chinook Pete (Kiel), discovers them and decides to replace his dead son with Lassie's master. Lassie runs away, finds the Mounties, and effects a rescue.
Sources: AFI Index, F6.2683; Copyright Registration, LP 26266. No film has been found.

55. *Violent Midnight* (Victoria Films, 1963), 93 min.
Synopsis: This mystery includes a deaf-mute chauffeur, who is one of four murder suspects.
Source: AFI Index, F6.5369. No film has been found.

56. *Hollywood Nudes Report* (Barry Mahon Productions, 1963), 64 min.
Synopsis: A publisher enters the nude movie business, and after interviewing several beautiful women, he selects a deaf-mute as his first star.
Source: AFI Index, F6.2172. No film has been found.

57. *Nine Miles to Noon* (Daron Enterprises, 1963), 67 min.
Synopsis: An American travels to Greece to find the wife and child he deserted years earlier. The wife has remarried and the American tries to convince his son to assist in the murder of his stepfather. The son's friend is a "deaf-mute."
Source: AFI Index, F6.3503. No film has been found.

58. *Casanova, '70* (Embassy, 1965), 4 reels, 16mm, color, sound. Producer: Carlo Ponti. Deaf character: Marco Ferreri.
Synopsis: *The Casanova of 1970 (Marcello Mastroianni) is impotent and can be aroused sexually only by danger. Accordingly, he woos the wife of a jealous aristocrat who feigns deafness and overhears his wife's plot to kill him. Although Casanova is only interested in the seduction of the wife, the old aristocrat is accidentally killed and the lover is accused of murder. Casanova is saved when it is proved that the victim was not deaf.
Source: Film Collection, LC.

59. *A Ballad of Love* (rel. in the USSR in 1965; Riga Films, 1966), sound. Director: Mikhail Bogin. Screenplay by Mikhail Bogin and Yuri Chulyukin. Deaf character: Victoria Fyodorova.
Synopsis: *Winner of a Moscow Festival short subject film award, this is an English-subtitled Russian love story about a hearing musician (Valentin Smirnitsky) and a dancer (Fyodorova) who has been deaf since the age of three as the result of an air-raid bombing. Natasha works at the circus, where she studies to be an acrobatic dancer, and at the pantomime theater for deaf-mutes, where she operates the lights. The scenes at the theater include the

production of *Romeo and Juliet,* with apparently authentic deaf actors speaking in Russian signs and finger spelling (hearing readers voice the dialogue). Although Natasha signs with her deaf friends, she reads Sergi's lips and writes notes. She asks him what music is like and explains that she can only remember the air-raid sounds and a lullaby; he invites her to his next concert, and in place of the music she hears the sounds of bombs and the lullaby.

Sources: Gallaudet University Film Collection, 745 (hereafter, GU Media); *New York Times Film Review* (February 21, 1966), 51:1.

60. *Mirage* (Universal, 1965), 12 reels, b&w, sound. Director: Edward Dmytrk.

Synopsis: *Several references mention deaf-blindness in connection with this film starring Gregory Peck; however, there are no deaf-blind or deaf characters. When Peck seeks escape from the police, a woman who refuses to give him refuge says, "I can't see or hear, I'm deaf and blind," and the script does take advantage of the audience's bias about hearing loss when an old man with a hearing aid turns out to be a professional killer.

Source: Film Collection, LC.

61. *Weekend of Fear* (J.D. Productions, 1966). Produced, directed, and script by Joe Danford. Deaf character: Kenneth Washman.

Synopsis: The actors do not speak in this low-budget film; narration is dubbed through a stream-of-consciousness device. The plot centers around a middle-aged woman who hires a deaf-mute to kill the girlfriend of the man she desires.

Source: Clippings, AMPAS. No film has been found.

62. *Who's Minding the Mint?* (Mauer Productions; dist., Columbia, 1967), 97 min.

Synopsis: This comedy centers on a plot to break into the U.S. Mint and print duplicate bills. A hard-of-hearing safecracker is a member of the gang.

Sources: AFI Index, F6.5559. Film Collection, LC.

63. *Psych-Out* (Dick Clark Enterprises, 1968), 12 reels, color, sound. Producer: Dick Clark. Director: Richard Rush. Deaf character: Susan Strasberg.

Synopsis: *This film depicts the life-style, music, and drug scene of San Francisco's flower children. A young, deaf runaway (Strasberg) who is searching for her brother speaks clearly, reads lips perfectly, and does not use sign language.

Source: Film Collection, LC.

64. *The Heart Is a Lonely Hunter* (Warner/Seven Arts, 1968), 12 reels, color, sound. Director: Robert E. Miller. Screenplay by Tom Ryan, based on a novel by Carson McCullers. Deaf characters: Alan Arkin, Chuck McCann, and a cameo appearance by deaf actor Horace Oats, Jr.

Synopsis: *The film deals with loneliness and alienation in a small southern town. The chief symbol of loneliness is a deaf jeweler, John Singer (Arkin), who remains mute but is an expert lip-reader; various townspeople discover that he is a good listener and tell him their troubles. Singer's only true friend is another deaf man, with whom he communicates freely through sign language; unlike Singer, who is intelligent, disciplined, and sensitive, Antonapoulos (McCann) is childlike and unable to satisfy his gluttonous appetite. When his deaf friend is sent to an institution for the mentally ill, where he eventually dies, Singer despairs and commits suicide. The signs and finger spelling used by Arkin and McCann are stiff, awkward, and often wrong; and since there is no voice interpretation, the hearing audience is not exposed to the poor communication quality. The only clear sign communication occurs in a brief scene where Singer helps the local black doctor speak with a deaf black patient (Oats).

Source: Film Collection, LC.

65. *Our Silent Love* (*Chichi To Ko*) (Toho Co., 1969), sound. Directed and original screenplay by Zenzo Matsuyama. Deaf character: unknown.

Synopsis: A young Japanese man, the son of deaf parents, cannot find employment. A factory owner, who has a deaf daughter, offers him a job and then tries to convince his daughter that if she marries her deaf lover instead of this young man she will have deaf children. The deaf couple attempt suicide but are saved, and the young man convinces the deaf woman to marry her deaf lover in spite of the parents' interference.

Source: AFI Index, F6.3678.

66. *Koshish* (N.P. Sippy, 1970), 4 reels, color, sound. Director and writer: Gulzar. Producers: Romu N. Sippy and Raj N. Sippy. Deaf characters: Jaya Bhadauri, Sanjeev Kumar.

Synopsis: *This Indian (Hindi) film depicts the life of a deaf man, Hari (Kumar), and a deaf woman, Aarti (Bhaduri). Aarti's mother uses homemade, primitive gestures with her; and her brother takes advantage of Aarti's deafness by stealing her possessions. Aarti meets Hari, who convinces her mother to send Aarti to the same school he attended for speech lessons and, more important, sign language. Although Aarti is worried about deaf children, she and Hari recognize their need for mutual support and marry. Their first child can hear but dies when he crawls out through an open door; their second child also can hear, and the couple takes in a blind man who serves as their ears for the child's cries. Many years later Aarti dies and Hari's boss proposes a marriage between his daughter, who is a deaf-mute, and Hari's son, Amit. Hari readily agrees but Amit refuses; he reconsiders, however, and the film closes with his finger-spelled proposal to Padma.

Source: GU Archives (no assigned media number).

67. *The Pleasure Game* (Wodwo Productions; dist., Eve Productions, 1970), 78 min.

Synopsis: An impotent father satisfies his sexual needs by watching others through peepholes. On one occasion he brings home two women, one of whom is deaf.

Source: AFI Index, F6.3858. No film has been found. For other examples of deaf characters in sex-oriented films, see *Hot Boarding House* (1970, AFI Index, F6.2217) and *Private Arrangement* (1970, AFI Index, F6.3924).

68. *Tarzan's Deadly Silence* (National General Pictures, 1970), 88 min.

Synopsis: Tarzan is temporarily deafened as the result of grenades thrown into a river while he is engaged in a fight.

Source: AFI Index, F6.4886.

69. *Fuzz* (Filmways; rel., United Artists, 1972), 10 reels, color, sound. Executive producer: Edward Feldman. Producer: Jack Farren. Director: Richard Colla. Screenplay by Evan Hunter (Ed McBain). Deaf characters: Neile Adams, Yul Brynner.

Synopsis: *This film depicts the success of the "inept" detectives of the 87th Precinct in solving three unrelated crimes (arson, robbery, and extortion). Two hearing-impaired characters are featured: Teddy Carella (Adams) is the deaf-mute wife of one of the detectives (she reads her husband's lips, remains silent, and uses a few awkward signs and finger spelling); the "deaf-man" (Brynner) is a murderer and extortionist who occasionally asks people to speak louder or to look at his face but has little difficulty with communication (he wears a hearing aid and makes all of his threats via the telephone).

Source: Film Collection, LC.

70. *Deaf Smith and Johnny Ears* (rel., MGM, 1973), sound. Producers: Joseph Janni and Luciano Perugia. Director: Paolo Cavara. Deaf character: Anthony Quinn.

Synopsis: In this Italian-made western, Quinn plays a deaf-mute war veteran who ekes out a living as a hired gun.

Source: MGM Pressbooks, LC. No film has been found.

71. *Harry in Your Pocket* (United Artists, 1973), color, sound. Producer and director: Bruce Geller. Written by James D. Buchanan and Ronald Austin. Deaf characters: Robert Peace, Arthur Horan, Margaret Horan, Don Peace, Carolyn Peace, Freda Harlander.

Synopsis: *Local deaf people are used in an opening scene at the Seattle-Takoma Airport, where they send off some friends on vacation. One of the deaf persons is the victim of a pickpocket.

Source: Film Collection, LC.

72. *Badlands* (1973), color, sound. Produced, directed, and written by Terrence Malick. Deaf character: Donna Baldwin.

Synopsis: *Martin Sheen and Sissy Spacek star in this film about a polite but amoral young man (Sheen) who shoots anyone who blocks his efforts to be with Holly (Spacek). She willingly accompanies him as he avoids pursuit by

police through several western states. In one scene they seek refuge and sup-
plies at a rich man's house, when the deaf maid allows them access to the
house (she is one of the few characters Kit does not shoot).
Source: Personal viewing.

73. *Tommy* (Columbia, 1975), 14 reels, color, sound. Producers: Robert
Stigwood and Kenneth Russell. Director: Kenneth Russell. Based on a rock
opera by "The Who" and Peter Townshend. Deaf character: Roger Daltrey.
Synopsis: *Tommy is a "deaf, dumb, and blind" character who becomes a
world champion pinball-machine player. His mother (Ann-Margret) takes
him to specialists, faith healers, and acid queens in search of a cure. Tommy
eventually is cured and becomes an evangelist in this vehicle for pop psy-
chology and rock music. No sign language or finger spelling is used during
the film; however, Tommy does give a gesture-song sermon to a congregation
seated in wheelchairs and they respond in a similar gesture-song. Unfortunately, it is all a parody of signs.
Source: Film Collection, LC.

74. *Nashville* (Paramount, 1975), 16 reels, color, sound. Producers: Jerry
Weintraub and Robert Altman. Director: Robert Altman. Script by Joan
Tewkesbary. Deaf characters: James Don Calvert and Donna Denton (both
deaf).
Synopsis: *This is a cynical look at the country music industry and individual
singers in Nashville. One of the leading characters is played by Lily Tomlin,
a gospel singer and the mother of two deaf children, both of whom use authentic Manual English and speak with hearing-impaired voices.
Source: Film Collection, LC.

75. *Against a Crooked Sky* (Doty-Dayton, 1975), 92 min., color, sound.
Producer: Lyman D. Dayton. Director: Earl Bellamy. Screenplay by Douglas
Stewart and Eleanor Lamb. Mute character: Henry Wilcoxon.
Synopsis: *A teenage girl is kidnapped by Indians and her brother teams up
with a feisty prospector (Richard Boone) and a mute Indian chief, Cut-
Tongue, who uses Indian sign language, to find her. In one scene the pros-
pector voice-interprets for the Indian. The signs are a mixture of obvious
Indian signs and an occasional sign borrowed from American Sign Language.
Source: Clippings, AMPAS.

76. *Looking for Mr. Goodbar* (Paramount, 1977), 15 reels, color, sound.
Producer: Freddie Fields. Directed and screenplay by Richard Brooks, based
on the novel by Judith Rossner. Deaf character: unknown local deaf children
and deaf adults.
Synopsis: *Diane Keaton stars as Theresa, a young woman raised in a traditional Catholic family, who, confronted with the unhappy marriages of her
parents and sister, and the knowledge that her own childhood curvature of the

spine is congenital, rejects marriage and children for herself. By day, Theresa is a competent teacher of deaf children; by night, she cruises the singles bars of Manhattan and meets several unsavory characters, one of whom ultimately kills her. There are numerous opportunities to observe signed English, interpreting, and speech pedagogy; and Manual English, speech, and amplification are each emphasized. Lou Fant (the son of deaf parents) appears briefly as an interpreter.

Source: Film collection, LC.

77. *Voices* (MGM, 1979), 12 reels, color, sound. Producer: Joe Wizan. Director: Robert Markowitz. Script by John Herzfeld. Deaf characters: Amy Irving, Richard Kendall (a deaf actor).

Synopsis: *Rosemarie Lemon (Irving), a deaf teacher of deaf children, is engaged to a deaf man (Kendall), but she meets and falls in love with a hearing man (Michael Ontkean), who aspires to be a successful singer. Rosemarie's mother (Viveca Lindfors) disapproves of this "mixed" courtship and advises Rosemarie to stay with her own kind (the deaf fiancé); she also advises Rosemarie to ignore her hearing boyfriend's encouragement to dance professionally. Irving and other hearing cast members use signed English correctly. The only scene in which the deaf boyfriend appears is brief and none of the signed conversation is translated for the audience; there is also an adult education scene that includes deaf adults who use American Sign Language. This is the first film in which an actor (Irving) attempts a hearing-impaired voice, which conveys the clear message that a deaf person can be intelligent, employed professionally, and happy but unable to speak like a person who hears. As a result of protests in California, MGM provided the first captioned version of a commercial film.

Source: Film Collection, LC.

78. *Amy* (Walt Disney, 1981), 6 reels, color, sound. Producers: Jerome Courtland and William R. Yates. Director: Vincent McEveety. Script by Noreen Stone. Deaf characters: Otto Rechenberg (deaf actor) and other unidentified deaf students from local California schools.

Synopsis: *The setting for this film is a residential school for deaf and blind children at the turn of the century. A young teacher, Amy (Jenny Agutter), deserts her husband and arrives at the school to establish an "articulation" program (speech and lip-reading). A young boy, Henry (Rechenberg), is infatuated with the beautiful new teacher. Although supported by the school superintendent (Lou Fant), Amy is opposed by the school matron (Nanette Fabray) and school board members who do not think that deaf people can talk or should hope to be integrated with hearing people. Amy eventually wins over the matron when she teaches Henry how to say "mother," thereby providing the boy and his blind mother with a method of communicating. Armed with a sense of purpose, Amy is able to reject her husband when he comes to take her home. With the presence of Fant (whose parents are deaf), Fabray (who has a history of hearing impairment), and real deaf children in the cast, it is not surprising that the signs and finger spelling are clear and correct.

Source: Film Collection, LC. A shorter captioned version, *Amy on the Lips,* is available through the Captioned Films for the Deaf loan program.

79. *Eyes of a Stranger* (Georgetown Productions; dist., Warner, 1981), 10 reels, color, sound. Director: Ken Wiederhorn. Script by Martin Jackson and Eric Bloom. Deaf-blind character: Jennifer Jason Leigh.

Synopsis: *A Miami television broadcaster becomes increasingly alarmed about a rapist who has murdered several local young women (her younger sister, Tracy [Leigh] is deaf, blind, and mute as a result of a childhood rape). Jane (Lauren Tewes) suspects that the killer (John DiSanti) lives in her apartment complex and tries to scare him off. In the end, the killer finds Tracy alone in the apartment and taunts and assaults her, which triggers the return of her hearing and sight. She finds a gun, wounds her assailant, then staggers into the bathroom, where she looks into the mirror and is fascinated by her own face and body. The killer attacks her again, but Jane arrives and shoots him in the head. The sisters embrace, and Tracy, having regained all of her senses, speaks her sister's name. The film successfully depicts an independent mute-deaf-blind woman, and the few scenes in which signs and finger spelling are used do so concisely and clearly.

Source: Film Collection, LC.

80. *The Boat Is Full* (Limbo Films, 1981), 100 min.

Synopsis: In this film, a German Jew feigns deafness to avoid expulsion from Switzerland to Germany.

81. *Black Moon Rising* (New World Pictures, 1986), color, sound. Producers: Douglas Curtis and Joel Michaels. Director: Harley Cokliss. Story and screenplay by John Carpenter. Deaf character: unknown.

Synopsis: *This is the story of the effort to steal and recover a high-tech automobile. One of the helpers of the car's owner is deaf, and he is killed when he cannot hear the villain's car approaching. Other than a few gestures, no signs are used.

Source: Videotape rental.

82. *Children of a Lesser God* (Paramount, 1986), color, sound. Producers: Burt Sugarman and Patrick Palmer. Director: Randa Haines. Screenplay by Hesper Anderson and Mark Medoff, based on the stage play by Mark Medoff. Deaf characters: Marlee Matlin, Linda Bove, William Byrd, Frank Carter, Jr., John Cleary, Georgia Ann Cline, Alison Gompf, Bob Hiltermann, Philip Holmes, and John Limnidis (all deaf).

Synopsis: *This love story involves a speech teacher (William Hurt) and a nonspeaking deaf woman (Matlin) who signs and is extremely suspicious of all persons who hear. All of the deaf characters either have understandable speech or are voice-interpreted by the teacher (Hurt), and the signs are authentic.

Source: Released for commercial distribution in 1986.

Television and Deafness

Since it is difficult to obtain access to individual television episodes, particularly those aired prior to the widespread use of videotape in the late 1960s, much of the information here has been reconstructed from print sources. When episodes have included a deaf character, they usually are reported in publications from the deaf community; even though such information is often sketchy, I have included the episodes for reference purposes because the standard indexes of television programming do not include deafness as a subject heading. Where I have found a single detailed and fairly complete account or synopsis of an episode, I have listed that as a source; otherwise, I list no source (the information has been reconstructed from a variety of publications: television references, deaf community newspapers, *Daily Variety* [Hollywood], and the *TV Guide*). An asterisk indicates that I have personally viewed the episode.

1. "Four Star Playhouse: Sound Off, My Love" (CBS, February 12, 1953), 30 min., b&w. Producer: Don Sharpe. Director: Robert Florey. Teleplay by John and Gwen Bagni. Deaf character: Merle Oberon.

Synopsis: Oberon plays a woman whose vanity prevents her from wearing a hearing aid. When she finally obtains one, she overhears a plot on her life by her husband (Gordon Oliver).

Source: *Daily Variety* (February 16, 1953), p. 8 (hereafter, *DV*).

2. "Tales of Tomorrow: The Great Silence" (ABC, February 1953), 30 min., b&w. Producer: George Foley, Jr. Deaf character: unknown.

Synopsis: An interplanetary blight wipes out speech among most of the earth's population. Burgess Meredith and his hillbilly mother communicate in sign language.

3. "Racket Squad: His Brother's Keeper" (CBS, 1953). Producer: Hal Roach, Jr. Director: Frank McDonald. Deaf character: unknown.

Synopsis: The episode deals with the deaf imposter racket.

4. "Big Town: Mute Justice" (NBC, March 18, 1954), 30 min. Script by Jerry Adelman. Deaf character: unknown.

Synopsis: A deaf-mute is hit by a truck when crossing the street. The case goes to court and everyone is surprised when the man admits he crossed against the red light. Reporters become suspicious, however, and discover that the court interpreter and the trucking company conspired to victimize the deaf man. V. A. Becker (a California rehabilitation counselor) served as the technical adviser.

Source: Copyright Registration, LU 3079.

5. "Lux Video Theater: Spent in Silence" (CBS, March 25, 1954), 30 min., b&w. Director: Buzz Kulik. Screenplay by Malvin Wald and Jack Jacobs. Deaf character: Nancy Olsen.

Synopsis: "Without a word of dialog," Olson portrays a deaf woman who wants love, not pity. Defying her father (Wilton Groff), who wants her to marry another mute, she falls in love with a hearing photographer (John Hudson).

Source: *DV* (March 29, 1954), p. 45.

6. "Pepsi-Cola Playhouse: The Sound of Silence" (ABC, April 23, 1954), 30 min., b&w. Producer: Revue. Director: Richard Irving. Teleplay by Lawrence Kimble. Deaf character: Sallie Brophy.

Synopsis: A wealthy father (Carl Reid) keeps his deaf daughter (Brophy) a virtual prisoner in their mansion because of his guilt over an auto accident that killed his wife and deafened their child. When an artist (Jack Kelly) comes to paint her portrait, they fall in love despite the father's objections.

Source: *DV* (April 26, 1954), p. 7.

7. "Medic: My Very Good Friend Albert" (NBC, November 27, 1954), 30 min., 16 mm, b&w. Director: Bernard Girard. Producer: Frank LaTourette. Deaf character: Robert Osterloh.

Synopsis: *Richard Boone narrates as Dr. Konrad Styner. A cello player and Swedish immigrant (Osterloh) loses his job with an orchestra because of otosclerosis. His naturalization class teacher advises him to see a doctor, who performs fenestration surgery and restores his hearing. Enjoying sound again, the cellist gets his job back and, with newfound confidence, asks an attractive classmate for a date.

Source: University of California, Los Angeles, Film, Television, and Radio Archives (hereafter, UCLA Archives).

8. "Big Story: Born—A Son" (NBC, June 17, 1955), 30 min., b&w. Deaf character: unknown.

Synopsis: Host Ben Grauer narrates this dramatization of a news story about a welfare agency's attempts to take the newborn son away from a blind and deaf Ohio couple, Harold and Georgia Hathaway. They appeal to a newspaper reporter, Helen Waterhouse, from the Akron *Beacon Journal*.

9. "Robert Montgomery Presents: There's No Need to Shout" (NBC, June 19, 1955), 60 min., b&w. Deaf character: Nancy Malone.

Synopsis: Writer Frances Warfield (Malone) becomes increasingly deaf, which causes her not to hear a proposal of marriage and leads her "almost to suicide." She at first rejects a hearing aid but eventually confronts her disability.

10. "Front Row Center: Johnny Belinda" (CBS, June 29, 1955), 60 min., b&w. Producer and director: Fletcher Markle. Adaptation by Leonard Freeman. Deaf character: Katherine Bard.

Synopsis: *In this live adaptation of the Broadway play, the emphasis on speech is reintroduced (compare to 1948 film version). Eddie Albert plays the doctor who promises that Belinda will "talk within a year." The execution of signs and finger spelling is generally poor, particularly by Albert.

Source: UCLA Archives.

11. "Alfred Hitchcock Presents: You Got to Have Luck" (CBS, January 15, 1956), 30 min., b&w. Deaf character: Marisa Pavan.

Synopsis: A villain (John Cassavetes) terrorizes a housewife and forces her to give his dictated answers over the telephone and also to turn away a friend at the door. The telephone caller is alerted to trouble (having expected the husband to answer) and calls the police, who captures the villain as he leaves the house. It turns out that the housewife is deaf and an excellent lip-reader.

Source: Copyright Registration, LP 6791.

12. "Screen Directors Playhouse: No. 5 Checked Out" (NBC, January 18, 1956), 30 min., b&w. Director: Ida Lupino. Deaf character: Teresa Wright.

Synopsis: *Mary (Wright), who is deaf and has worked in the village school as a teacher of lip-reading, remains at her father's mountain motel while he visits a sick brother. Recently jilted because of her deafness, she worries that she will never marry and raise a family. An excellent lip-reader who speaks naturally, Mary unknowingly rents one of the cabins to a pair of bank robbers, Willy (Peter Lorre) and Barney (William Tallman). Upset that his partner shot and killed a bank customer, Barney wants to abandon his life of crime and befriends Mary so he can steal her car and escape. Barney takes Mary's car key but returns to save her from Willy, who is intent on killing her because he believes Mary overheard an incriminating conversation and refuses to believe Barney's explanation that she is deaf. Mary sits on a river bank, fishing, oblivious to the sound of gunfire behind her as the two bank robbers kill each other.

Sources: Copyright Registration, LP 7485; UCLA Archives.

13. "The Listening Hand" (ABC, March 6, 1956), 30 min., b&w. Deaf characters: Barbara Eiler, John Craven.

Synopsis: See TV no. 8. The deaf-blind couple in this dramatization are also called the Hathaways.

14. "Loretta Young Show: Double Partners" (NBC, August 26, 1956), 30 min., 16 mm, b&w. Producer: John London. Script by William Bruckner. Deaf character: Loretta Young.

Synopsis: *Austin and Ruth (Young) Baxter are attorneys; Ruth is deaf. One night alone in her office, she is confronted by a villain searching for a man, Planchek, who is hiding. Ruth shields Planchek but she is not able to read his lips because he has a foreign accent. A grenade is tossed into her office and Planchek saves her life, losing his own. A crooked politican, Craigie, is suspected as the employer of the villain but Ruth's husband cannot believe that Craigie is a crook and courts him for legal business. Craigie meets his clients on a park bench below Ruth's law office window, and with the aid of binoculars she reads his lips and concludes that he did hire the killer. In the end, her husband realizes his misplaced trust in Craigie and rescues Ruth from an attack. Young's portrayal of a deaf person on television is consistent with her movie portrayals.

Sources: Copyright Registration, LP 9625; UCLA Archives.

15. "Playhouse 90: The Miracle Worker" (CBS, February 7, 1957), 60 min., b&w. Teleplay by William Gibson, based on *The Story of My Life* by Helen Keller. Deaf character: Patty McCormack.

Synopsis: *See the description of the 1962 film version (no. 53).

Source: Museum of Broadcasting, New York, T77:0111,12.

16. "Schlitz Playhouse: The Life You Save" (CBS, March 1, 1957), 30 min., b&w. Producer: Frank P. Rosenberg. Director: Herschel Daugherty. Teleplay by Nelson Gidding, based on story by Flannery O'Connor. Deaf character: Janice Rule.

Synopsis: Tom Triplet (Gene Kelly) is a one-armed tramp who stops by a southern farmhouse and offers to fix things in exchange for room and board. Mrs. Crater (Agnes Moorehead) agrees and tries to convince Triplet to marry her angelic deaf-mute daughter, Lucynell (Rule). Triplet marries her but is unhappy about it and abandons her. He sees a sign, "The Life You Save May Be Your Own," counsels a runaway boy to return to his parents, and returns himself to Lucynell. Out of love and gratitude she articulates his first name.

Source: Copyright Registration, LP 8365.

17. "Frontiers of Faith: Song Out of Silence" (NBC, 1957?), 30 min., b&w. Script by Bernard S. Reines. Technical adviser: Dorothy Kraft of the Lexington School for the Deaf. Deaf characters: Guy Sorell, Joyce Ebert.

Synopsis: *Charles Van Doren introduces and narrates the story of Thomas H. Gallaudet's successful effort to establish the first American school for the deaf in Hartford, Connecticut. Gallaudet (Ray Boyle) travels to Europe where he meets a French deaf teacher, Laurent Clerc (Sorell), who collaborates in the establishment of the American school and the introduction of the one-handed manual alphabet into the United States. Gallaudet's deaf wife, Sophia, is played by Joyce Ebert.

Source: GU Media 820.

18. "Panic [aka "No Warning"]: Hear No Evil" (NBC, April 13, 1958). Deaf character: Mercedes McCambridge.

Synopsis: Helen Colby (McCambridge) loses her hearing when her only child dies in an accident. She obtains a hearing-aid comb that restores her hearing

and is about to share the news with her husband on their wedding anniversary when she overhears her husband and her sister plot her death. They sedate her and leave her in a car parked on a railroad track, but she slips out at the last minute and confronts her husband when the police investigate the wreck of the abandoned car.
Source: Copyright Registration, LP 12818.

19. "Hallmark Hall of Fame: Johnny Belinda" (NBC, October 13, 1958), 90 min., b&w. Producer and director: George Schaefer. Adapted by Theodore Apstein, based on the play by Elmer Harris. Deaf character: Julie Harris.
Synopsis: *See the description of the 1948 film (no. 30). This version is closer to the stage play in its emphasis on lip-reading and speech. Even though the prospects of a successful articulation program for an English illiterate deaf adult are virtually nil, the possibility exists throughout the story. Despite the emphasis on articulation, Harris's signs and finger spelling are well executed. In contrast, her teacher, Dr. Pelletier (Christopher Plummer), who speaks with a French accent, uses signs that are consistently awkward from beginning to end.
Source: Museum of Broadcasting, T85–0053,54. For further information, see "Julie Harris Visits Gallaudet College" (Gallaudet, 1958), 4 min. (16mm), b&w, sound (GU Archives 57).

20. "Silents Please: The Clown Princes of Hollywood" (Gregton Enterprises, Sterling Education Film Release, 1959), 1 reel, 16mm, b&w, silent, captioned. Producer: Paul Killian. Deaf character: unknown.
Synopsis: *This is a film compilation of silent film comedians; it appears periodically on television. Interpretive comments have been added to the silent film clips, one of which is *Kill or Cure* (1923), featuring Stan Laurel before he teamed up with Oliver Hardy. Laurel plays a salesman who delivers his spiel to a prospect, with no effect. The reason is made clear when another man arrives who communicates in signs and the two men leave, revealing that the post Laurel's prospect was leaning against holds a sign that reads "Deaf and Dumb Institute." A woman arrives and Laurel decides to "sign" to her in a parody of sign language. She attacks him, and the scene ends in a chase. The interpretive comment notes that the public of the silent era was insensitive to this parody of the disabled.
Source: Film Collection, LC; Video Images, "Stan without Ollie: Volume I," Videoyesteryear Recording; GU Media, 1145.

21. "Dupont Show with June Allyson: A Silent Panic" (CBS, December 22, 1960), 30 min. Script by Arthur Dales. Deaf character: Harpo Marx.
Synopsis: Dummy Taylor (Marx) has a job as the "mechanical man" in a department store (crowds guess whether he is a man or a robot). Because he cannot read, speak, read lips, or use sign language, when he sees someone shoot a person in the crowd with a silenced pistol, the police are frustrated in

their inability to understand him. On his way to work one day, he spots the killer and he flees, hiding in a lumber yard. Discovered by the night watchman, the two men develop a bond. The killer arrives but the night watchman will not divulge the dummy's hiding place. The dummy manages to sneak off and returns with the police, who save his new friend.

Source: Copyright Registration, LP 19535.

22. *Lassie: A Joyous Sound* (NBC, 1960), 3 reels, 16mm, color. Producers: Bonita Granville Wrather and William Beaudine, Jr. Directors: Jack Hively, Jack Wrather, and Dick Mader. Script by Robert Schaeffer and Eric Frelwald. Deaf character: Pamelyn Ferdin (?).

Synopsis: *In this television movie, Lassie's young mistress, Lucie, is deaf, a difficulty "she has suffered . . . with courage and dignity." Although she speaks naturally and reads lips perfectly, her mother still hopes for a cure and takes her to the big city to visit one more doctor, who explains that Lucie has conductive deafness, or otosclerosis, and that she is a good candidate for surgery. After the operation, Lucie still does not hear, but the doctor explains that perhaps her hearing will return when the swelling recedes. In the interim, Lassie becomes separated from the family, but after several adventures she finds her way home. Walking in a nearby field, Lucie begins to hear sounds, including the sound of Lassie's bark, and the two are tearfully reunited.

Source: Film Collection, LC.

23. "Checkmate Suspense: The Deadly Silence" (CBS, April 8, 1961). Deaf character: Diana Lynn.

Synopsis: This is the story of a deaf teacher of deaf children who is threatened by criminals and protected by San Francisco private detectives.

Source: Copyright Registration, LP 20610.

24. "87th Precinct" (NBC, 1961). Deaf character: Gena Rowlands.

Synopsis: Detective Steve Carella (Robert Lansing) is married to a deaf-mute woman. Deaf publications commented that she never used sign language.

25. "Dick Powell Playhouse: Rage of Silence" (NBC, January 29, 1963), 60 min., b&w. Director: Don Taylor. Teleplay by Ed Spiegel and Jules Maitland. Deaf characters: Carol Lynley, Peter Falk.

Synopsis: The story involves Elise (Lynley), who is very outgoing and expressive in the use of sign language, and a student in the adult education class she teaches (Falk), who is also deaf but is unable to express himself in speech or signs and quick to anger. Elise befriends Martin, but he misunderstands her kindness and becomes jealous of her hearing boyfriend. He is eventually killed by the police as he attempts to drown Elise's boyfriend. Elise cries for Martin and his inability to communicate. The *Daily Variety* review was very critical of Falk's performance as overly violent.

Source: Copyright Registration, LP 30427.

26. "Ben Casey: A Woods Full of Question Marks" (NBC, October 26,

1964), 60 min., b&w. Deaf character: June Reed (a student from the Mary E. Bennett School for Deaf in Los Angeles).

Synopsis: Dr. Casey (Vincent Edwards) performs emergency surgery and later discovers that his patient is deaf. The father (Dane Clark) wants to send his daughter, Kathy, to a school for mentally retarded children, since he thought she had been attending special schools but was not making any progress (the money was being spent on the girl's alcoholic mother). He relents and sends Kathy to a school for deaf, and after two weeks she pronounces the word "ball." Her father is now convinced that she will eventually learn to communicate.

Source: Copyright Registration, LP 31420.

27. "Slattery's People: How Sweet Are Unheard Melodies" (CBS, Fall 1965). Deaf character: June Reed.

Synopsis: Unknown, but the series features a state representative who champions the underdog.

28. "Lassie: The Day the Mountain Shook" (CBS, April 6 or 14, 1966), 30 min., color. Producer: Robert Golden. Director: Jack B. Hively. Script by Robert Schaefer and Eric Freiwald. Deaf characters: oral-deaf boys from the Mary E. Bennett School, including Ronald Kleiger, Jeffry Dichter, Jeffrey Rees, Beau Baker, and Matthew Brandfield.

Synopsis: *While at a summer camp for oral-deaf boys who communicate through lip-reading and speech, Joey (who became deaf after surviving an automobile wreck in which his parents died) finds an injured squirrel, which he nurses back to health. When he tries to return the squirrel to the woods, Joey becomes lost and takes shelter in a cave; an earthquake traps him inside and he passes out. As Lassie and the boys' camp supervisor, Corey, search for Joey, Lassie hears the squirrel and follows him to the cave. Corey digs Joey out and carries him to safety. The boy is revived and, hearing the sounds of the squirrel and Lassie, says "I . . . I can hear. . . ." No signs are used in the episode, and early scenes establish the fact that all of the boys attend an oral education program and will be "normal" when they graduate from high school. The adult supervisors comment that in earlier days these boys would have been placed in institutions.

Source: Copyright Registration, LP 33806.

29. "NBC Special: Experiment in Television" (NBC, April 2, 1967). Deaf characters: National Theatre of the Deaf.

Synopsis: This was the first nationally televised appearance of the newly created repertory company of deaf and hearing actors. There were dramatic readings as well as songs from the popular musical *Guys and Dolls*.

30. "ABC Color Special: Johnny Belinda" (ABC, October 22, 1967). Producer: David Susskind. Director: Paul Bogart. Adapted by Allen Sloan. Deaf character: Mia Farrow.

Synopsis: This is another version of the stage play; see also film no. 30; TV nos. 10, 19. Contemporary reviews of Farrow's performance were negative. Videotape copies of the performance have not been located.

31. "Mannix: The Silent Cry" (CBS, September 28, 1968), 60 min., color. Producers: Ivan Goff and Ben Roberts. Director: Don Taylor. Teleplay by Arthur Weiss. Deaf character: Audree Norton (a deaf actress).

Synopsis: Norton plays a deaf actress who lip-reads a conversation about a kidnapping. Mannix (Mike Connors) takes her case when her ability to lip-read makes her a target for murder. During the show Norton performs a sign-reading of Elizabeth Barrett Browning's "How Do I Love Thee?"; a *Daily Variety* reviewer observed that the poem's effect was lost because the camera kept switching from Norton to the interpreter to Connors. Norton's performance was the first by a deaf adult actor on a network series.

Source: *DV* (October 1, 1968), p. 18.

32. "Family Affair: The Language of Love" (CBS, January 29, 1970), 30 min., 16mm, color. Script by Charles Barton. Technical adviser: Faye Wilke. Deaf character: Audree Norton (a deaf actress), Diane Holly.

Synopsis: *Uncle Bill (Brian Keith) seeks help for his niece's (Anissa Jones) deaf friend, Juanita (Holly), whose mother does not want her to go to school. Uncle Bill visits a special school where he meets Dr. Robinson (Norton), an alumna and a teacher of lip-reading, who is mute and communicates by writing notes and reading lips. She convinces the mother to let Juanita attend school when the deaf girl successfully reads lips after a two-minute speech lesson.

Source: UCLA Archives.

33. "Marcus Welby, M.D.: Sounding Brass" (ABC, December 1, 1970), 60 min., color. Executive producer: David Victor. Producer: David O'Connell. Written by John Vlahos. Deaf character: Julian Weiss (a student at the Mary E. Bennett School for the Deaf).

Synopsis: An abused child (Weiss) whose family thinks he is retarded is taken to see Drs. Welby (Robert Young) and Kiley (James Brolin). The doctors take the mother and child to visit a hearing and speech clinic—the John Tracy Clinic in Los Angeles—where viewers are introduced to the basics of audiology and speech training. The boy, Billy, is fitted for a hearing aid, and his mother is impressed by his future possibilities and the need for her own hard work in speech and language therapy. Initially hostile, jealous, and filled with shame, the father finally comes around when Dr. Welby informs him that his son's deafness was probably caused by a blow to the head. The father goes to the clinic and the family joins together, determined to overcome deafness. In an epilogue, Welby and Kiley discuss the possibility of microsurgery to restore Billy's hearing but choose not to mention it to the family since they have taken the first step and made an adjustment to and accepted their son's deafness. This episode won recognition by the Alexander Graham Bell Association for its public service and educational value.

34. "Sesame Street" (PBS, April 1971). Deaf character: Linda Bove (a deaf actress).
Synopsis: A deaf character joins this educational children's program.

35. "The Man and the City: Hands of Love" (ABC, September 11, 1971), 60 min., color. Producer: Stanley Rubin. Director: Daniel Petrie. Teleplay by Bess Boyle. Deaf characters: Audree Norton (a deaf actress), Lou Fant (son of deaf parents).
Synopsis: *Mayor Alcala (Anthony Quinn) becomes interested in a deaf couple who want to adopt a hearing child placed in their home as a foster child. After initially refusing the placement recommended by the social worker (June Lockhart), the mayor goes to court and makes an impassioned plea on behalf of the boy, who has found the love he needs from the deaf couple. The plot parallels the 1966–67 Christensen adoption case in California, in which the state courts ruled that deaf people could adopt children.
Source: Film Collection, LC.

36. "The Waltons: The Foundling" (CBS, September 14, 1972), 60 min., color. Producer: Lorimar. Director: Vincent Sherman. Script by John Mc-Greevey. Deaf character: Erica Hunton.
Synopsis: *A father wants to put his uncommunicative, deaf daughter, Holly (Hunton), into an asylum, but his wife instead leaves the child on the Waltons' doorstep. The family takes care of her, and when they learn that she is deaf, John Boy (Richard Thomas) teaches her to finger spell. Holly helps rescue Elizabeth, who is trapped inside a trunk located in an abandoned shack, and her father, who has come to take her to an asylum, realizes that she is not retarded. All of the Walton children and Holly finger spell.
Source: Film Collection, LC; GU Media 678.

37. "Medical Center: Wall of Silence" (CBS, April 4, 1973), 60 min., color. Producer: Al Ward. Director: Paul Stanley. Written by Robert M. Young. Deaf characters: Kristoffer Tabori, Judy Strangis.
Synopsis: *A deaf teenager (Tabori) is injured and is taken to the Medical Center, where his doctor (Chad Everett) becomes convinced that Kyle's deafness is hysterical in nature. Kyle's father believes that his son has been disappointed too many times and refuses to cooperate. A deaf girlfriend, Cindy (Strangis), who speaks normally and lip-reads expertly, tells the doctor that she doesn't miss her hearing but realizes that she may have "taught" Kyle to be deaf. Kyle's stepmother confronts him with the fact that he lost his hearing only when she made physical advances. The admission triggers his memory and Kyle recovers his hearing.
Sources: Film Collection, LC; GU Media 65.

38. "Search for Tomorrow" (NBC series, initial appearance in 1973), 30 min., color. Deaf character: Linda Bove (a deaf actress).

Synopsis: In what was television's longest-running soap opera, Bove appeared as Melissa Hayley, who was taken in by one of the main characters, Joanne. Haley, who worked at Henderson Hospital, lost her hearing in a car accident and during her recovery fell in love with a doctor whose mother was deaf.

39. "NBC Special: A Child's Christmas in Wales" (NBC, December, 1973). Producer: Joshua White. Director: Robert Weiner. Narrated by Sir Michael Redgrave. Translator: Bernard Bragg. Deaf characters: actors from the National Theatre of the Deaf.

Synopsis: This was a Christmas program performed by the deaf repertory company.

40. "Marcus Welby, M.D.: Child of Silence" (ABC, June 17, 1975), 60 min., color. Producer: David O'Connell. Director: John Erman. Written by Jean Holloway. Deaf character: Cara Theresa Anderson.

Synopsis: *A young deaf girl (Anderson) who almost drowns is taken to Dr. Welby (Robert Young), who discovers that she has no regular physician. (The mother tells Dr. Welby that her own younger brother was born deaf and hated their father for dragging him from doctor to doctor in search of a cure; hence, she resists all efforts to check into her daughter's deafness.) When the daughter is nearly killed by an oncoming car, the mother agrees to an operation (for artresia—blockage of the middle ear), which is successful. The mother (Lois Nettleton) uses ASL with the daughter, and Dr. Welby uses a variety of communication devices, including mouthing, gestures, and a few signs. Actor Lou Fant (son of deaf parents) makes a cameo appearance as a store clerk; he may have served as a technical adviser even though his name is not listed in the credits as such.

Source: GU Media 503.

41. "Harry O: Silent Kill" (ABC, October 8, 1975), 60 min., color. Producers: Buck Houghton and Robert Dozier. Director: Richard Lang. Written by Stephan Kandel, based on a story by John Lucas. Deaf characters: James Wainwright, Kathy Lloyd.

Synopsis: *Ken Corby (Wainwright), a deaf man who uses signs and does not read lips, has been fired from his job as a janitor and is the prime suspect in an arson and murder case. His deaf wife (Lloyd), who speaks in an impaired voice and uses signs, hires private detective Harry Orwell (David Janssen) to prove his innocence. In several scenes, Lloyd has an opportunity to explain about the different kinds of deafness and deaf people. One scene depicts Ken's misunderstanding of a conversation between his wife and Orwell, which leads him to conclude that Orwell is personally interested in his

wife; since she often does not continue to sign when she speaks to Orwell, this is understandable. The hearing audience is also excluded from some of the signed dialogue for these scenes. Lou Fant (son of deaf parents) appears briefly as a court-assigned interpreter; presumably he functioned as technical adviser to the actors, whose sign skills clearly mark them as hearing persons.
Source: GU Media 686.

42. "Good Times" (CBS, November 11, 1975), 30 min., color. Producer: Jack Elinson and Norman Paul. Director: Herb Kenwith. Script by Roger Shulman and John Baskin. Deaf character: J. A. Preston.
Synopsis: *Willona (Ja'net Du Bois) is interested in Walter Ingles (Preston), who owns his own machine shop and happens to be deaf. Both Willona and Walter are happy to learn that neither is interested in marriage. Walter, who has been deaf for one year, lip-reads perfectly and occasionally uses signs, which provides an opportunity for the one-liner jokes typical of the show. CBS previewed this episode before a deaf audience and made a captioned videotape available for limited use.
Source: GU Media 821.

43. "Baretta: Shoes" (ABC, October 27, 1976), 60 min., color. Deaf character: Charlie Martin Smith.
Synopsis: *Police are baffled by a rapist-murderer who somehow convinces his victims to go off with him. A deaf shoeshine boy (Smith), who others refer to as "dummy"—Baretta (Robert Blake) calls him "Shoes"—witnesses the attempted rape of a local mission worker. "Shoes" cannot communicate (speech or signs), but he knows that the rapist has a police badge; Baretta finally figures it out. Together they save the mission worker, and the episode ends with "Shoes" and the mission worker going to school to learn to communicate.
Source: GU Media 978.

44. "Starsky and Hutch" (ABC, June 1976), 60 min., color. Producer: Joseph Naar. Director: George McCowan. Teleplay by Parke Perine, based on a story by Donald Boyle. Deaf characters: Chuck McCann and an unknown actor.
Synopsis: *Starsky (Paul Michael Glaser) and Hutch (David Soul) arrest Larry (McCann), a deaf-mute, for stealing candy. Their investigation reveals that Larry and another deaf friend, RC (unknown), are ex-cons whose former residence, a halfway house, is linked to a suspected murderer who also has staged several robberies (he masquerades as the priest who manages the residence). Larry is portrayed as a childlike "dummy"; when Starsky and Hutch save him from the murderer, they search toy stores, playgrounds, and pet stores, only to find him at a "kiddy matinee all-cowboy movie." The lip-reading is exaggerated and the few signs used are primitive.
Source: GU Media 919.

45. "Westside Medical: The Sound of Sunlight" (ABC, March 15, 1977), 60 min., color. Producer: Alan Armer. Director: Ralph Senesky. Script by Worley Thorne. Deaf characters: Nan Cousins, Jane Wilk (a deaf actress).

Synopsis: *A deaf child is injured in a playground accident and his deaf teacher (Cousins) accompanies him to the hospital. She remains with the boy because he distrusts hearing people. During the medical history interview, the doctors realize that the deaf teacher reacts to sound. Born deaf of deaf parents, she is reluctant to undergo an operation and consults her school principal (Wilk), who is also deaf. She finally agrees to surgery and asks if the sunlight will hurt her ears since it blinds your eyes when you look at it directly. When her hearing is restored, she has a difficult time adjusting to the hearing world and later tells the principal that what is important is "not hearing but knowing who I am." Except for Jane Wilk and cameo appearances by deaf children and an ASL teacher, the characters who use signs and finger spelling do so awkwardly.

Source: GU Media 1137.

46. "The Hardy Boys/Nancy Drew Mysteries: Mystery of the Silent Scream" (ABC, November 27, 1977), 60 min., color. Deaf character: unknown.

Synopsis: The Hardy boys are the only ones who believe a deaf-mute girl who lip-reads a plan to plant a bomb in a Las Vegas casino.

47. "ABC Afterschool Special: Mom and Dad Can't Hear Me" (ABC, 1978), 60 min., color. Producer: Daniel Wilson. Director: Larry Eliksaan. Deaf characters: Priscilla Pointer, Stephen Elliott.

Synopsis: *Charlie (Rosanna Arquette) and her family have recently moved to a new city, where her father (Elliott) works as a printer and her mother (Pointer) works at a local school for deaf children. She is reluctant to talk to her new friends at school about her parents' deafness and goes so far as to tell her friends that her mother is the family's maid. When she realizes what she has done, Charlie recants and screams hysterically that her parents use signs and that "we're all freaks." She runs away but eventually confesses to her parents, who understand and forgive her. In the end, they all go to a party to meet her friends. Although the signs are extremely awkward and implausible, the parents depict credible deaf speech, and incidental information about telecommunication devices and the parents' work is accurate and sympathetic. Deaf actress Audree Norton and her deaf husband auditioned for the role of the parents and, when turned down, alleged discrimination by the director and producer. Gabriel Grayson, a teacher of ASL and the hearing son of deaf parents, served as adviser.

Source: Film Collection, LC.

48. "James at 15: Actions Speak Louder" (NBC, January 31, 1978), 60 min., color. Director: Joseph Hardy. Teleplay by Ronald Rubin, based on

story by Paul Hudson. Deaf character: Kevin Van Wieringer (a deaf actor). Synopsis: *Over the objections of Scott's mother, James convinces his deaf friend (Van Wieringer) to transfer to his school. The pedantic plot allows for dialogue about mainstreaming issues and the ability of a deaf person to achieve in a regular school setting. Dramatic highlights include Scott's interaction with an insensitive girl and James's efforts to convince the soccer coach to allow Scott to play on the school team. Van Wieringer's portrayal is authentic; he communicates through Manual English, ASL, and occasional speech. A fellow deaf actor, Gregg Brooks, served as technical adviser. Source: GU Media 1214.

49. "The American Girls" (CBS, September 30, 1978), 60 min., color. Deaf character: unknown.

Synopsis: The first episode of this short-running series featured a deaf-mute aide to a camp director who hides an actress wanted for murder. The American Girls are investigative reporters who infiltrate the camp in search of the murderess.

50. . . . *And Your Name Is Jonah* (CBS, January 28, 1979), 120 min., color. Director: Richard Michaels. Script by Michael Bortman. Deaf characters: Jeffry Bravin, Bernard Bragg, Barbara Bernstein, and Billy Seago (all deaf actors).

Synopsis: *The Corellis (Sally Struthers and James Woods) bring their young son, Jonah (Bravin), home from a three-year stint at a facility for the mentally retarded after he is diagnosed as deaf, not retarded. Jonah makes no progress in an oral education program and, out of frustration, Woods abandons the family. Eventually, Struthers meets a deaf couple (Bragg and Bernstein) who introduce her to other deaf adults and to sign language. A deaf adult, Woody (Seago), breaks through the communication barrier with Jonah when he shows him that his favorite treat, a hot dog, has a sign. In the end, Struthers takes Jonah to a new school where they use Manual English, and when a little girl asks Jonah his name, he finger spells it and miraculously pronounces it too. Bragg also served as technical adviser, with credits to Gregg Brooks and the Alliance of Deaf Artists. Source: GU Media 1307.

51. *Dummy* (CBS, 1979), 120 min., color. Producer: Warner Bros. TV. Director: Frank Perry. Story by Ernest Tidyman. Deaf characters: Paul Sorvino, LeVar Burton, Joe Clark.

Synopsis: *This made-for-television movie recounts the legal saga of an illiterate deaf black man, Donald Lang (Burton), who was accused of murdering two prostitutes in Chicago. Lang's hearing-impaired attorney, Lowell Myers (Sorvino), pursues the constitutional question of whether the state has the right to confine a deaf person to jail or to a mental health facility when that person is neither insane nor found guilty of a crime (because he was legally

incompetent—unable to understand the accusation or help in his own defense). Lang has no formal communication system and uses primitive gestures; his lawyer uses some signs and finger spelling but functions primarily through lip reading (his sister, who functions as his secretary, interprets orally for him). The movie is narrated in a speech-impaired voice.
Source: GU Media 2043.

52. "Lou Grant" (CBS, January 1, 1979), 60 min., color. Deaf character: unknown.
Synopsis: Grant (Ed Asner), whose grandson is losing his hearing, helps his daughter cope with her child's deafness and her failing marriage.

53. *Silent Victory: The Kitty O'Neill Story* (CBS, February 24, 1979), 120 min., color. Producer: R. J. Louis. Director: Lou Antonio. Script by Stephen Gethers. Deaf character: Stockard Channing, Angelique and Elkin Antonio.
Synopsis: *Based on the real-life biography of deaf stuntwoman Kitty O'Neill, this television movie is an excellent example of the disabled person as superwoman. O'Neill plays the piano (*Chopsticks*), competes at the Olympic diving trials, and wards off a would-be rapist with her karate skills. Having successfully learned to speak and read lips as a child, O'Neill struggles to break her dependency on her mother and evolve her own life and career. When her mother dies, O'Neill resolves to set new land speed records to earn funds for "Listening with Your Eyes" schools, established by her mother to promote speech and lip-reading. In the final scene, a deaf girl signs (untranslated for the audience) "I love you," to which Kitty responds, "No, no" and holds the girl's arms while telling her to "talk." In an impaired voice, the girl says "Kitty."
Source: GU Media.

54. "The Love Boat: Sounds of Silence" (ABC, March 17, 1979), 60 min., color. Deaf character: unknown.
Synopsis: A musician falls in love with a deaf passenger.

55. *The Miracle Worker* (NBC, October 14, 1979), 120 min., color. Deaf character: Melissa Gilbert.
Synopsis: *This television movie of the William Gibson play based on Helen Keller's autobiography differs little from the 1962 film version (see no. 53)—except that Patty Duke Astin, who earlier played Keller, now plays Anne Sullivan. IBM and the National Association of the Deaf distributed 500,000 copies of the script to schools and libraries.
Source: Film Collection, LC.

56. "White Shadow" (CBS, October 15, 1979), 60 min. Deaf character: Glenn-Michael Jones.
Synopsis: A deaf transfer student tries out for the basketball team.
Source: *TV Guide.*

57. "Little House on the Prairie: Silent Promises" (NBC, January 28,

1980), 60 min., color. Deaf character: Alban Branton. Synopsis: Laura (Melissa Gilbert) learns signs and teaches them to a deaf friend, Daniel (Branton), and his father (Lou Fant, son of deaf parents).

58. *The Wild and the Free* (Marble Arch Productions, 1980), 100 min., color. Director: James Hill.
Synopsis: *This television movie is one of the first to take advantage of the publicity attached to primate research and sign communication. Granville Van Dusen plays a research scientist who takes his chimps to a wildlife refuge in Africa, where he is confronted by another scientist (Linda Gray) who accuses him of turning his "signing" chimps into pets. The two are reconciled when the "signing" chimps save wild chimps and the scientists from poachers. In general, the finger spelling and occasional signs executed by the human actors are correct; the chimps merely wave their arms in the air.
Source: Personal viewing.

59. "Barney Miller" (ABC, February 12, 1981), 30 min., color. Director: Noam Pitlik. Script by Paul Mauldin. Deaf characters: Phyllis Frelich, Seymour Bernstein, Peter Wechsberg (all deaf actors).
Synopsis: *Detective Dietrich (Steve Landesberg) arrests an attractive deaf prostitute (Frelich), which leads to several communication gags, such as, "Do you want me to mime her her rights?" Officer Levitt (Ron Carey) has a deaf sister and knows sign language, so he serves as interpreter. The prostitute is booked and in the process charms Dietrich. Her deaf lawyer (Bernstein) arrives to arrange bail, followed by her deaf pimp (Wechsberg). As she leaves the precinct, she reminds Dietrich that they have a date the next night, prompting Levitt to again offer his services as interpreter. The deaf actors all use ASL, and the deaf attorney character uses Manual English as well. Although the audience can understand most sign sequences through Levitt's interpreting, there are a few signed dialogues between the lawyer and Levitt that keep the hearing audience in the dark. Other than this communication problem, the deaf actors bring credibility to the episode.
Source: GU Media 1705.

60. "Fantasy Island: Chorus Girl" (ABC, February 21, 1981), 60 min., color. Deaf character: Lisa Hartman.
Synopsis: A dance teacher wants his deaf pupil to hear.

61. *The Second Family Tree* (NBC, March 1981). Producer: Carroll Newman. Director: Randa Haines. Deaf character: Johnny Kovacs (a deaf actor).
Synopsis: Two divorced individuals (Anne Archer and Frank Converse) live together in an extended family, with a deaf child. This television movie served as a pilot for a series.

62. "Nurse" (CBS, April 16, 1981), 60 min., color. Deaf characters: David Purdham, Elizabeth Quinn.
Synopsis: A deaf hospital employee (Purdham) reacts strangely when told

that his hearing can be restored. He is concerned that it would threaten his relationship with a deaf woman (Quinn).

63. "Trapper John, M.D.: The Albatross" (CBS, May 10, 1981), 60 min., color. Deaf character: Kathy Wiberg (a deaf actress).
Synopsis: Gonzo (Gregory Harrison) treats a sick deaf-mute girl who is inexplicably malnourished.

64. "Happy Days: Allison" (ABC, 1981), 30 min., color. Deaf character: Linda Bove (a deaf actress).
Synopsis: A deaf woman has a fling with the Fonz (Henry Winkler).

65. "Little House on the Prairie, a New Beginning: The Wild Boy" (NBC, 1982), 120 min., color. Producer: Kent McCray. Director: Victor French. Developed by Blanche Hanalis. Written by Vince Gutierrez. Mute character: Jonathan H. Kovacs (a deaf actor).
Synopsis: *This is the story of a mute boy (Kovacs) who is abused and displayed by a medicine show operator, Dr. McQueen (Anthony Zerbe). The children of Walnut Grove discover that the wild boy, who has escaped, is simply mute and that his behavior is the result of addiction to morphine, which is supplied by his "guardian." Mr. Edwards (Victor French) takes care of Matthew, and the town doctor discovers that the boy is mute because he swallowed lye. Laura (Melissa Gilbert) teaches all the characters signs and finger spelling so that Matthew will have a method of communication. Although McQueen returns to claim the boy, the community prevails and Matthew is allowed to remain with Mr. Edwards. The episode is unique in that a mute who hears is played by a deaf actor.
Source: GU Media.

66. *Hear No Evil* (CBS, 1982), 120 min., color. Deaf character: Gil Gerard.
Synopsis: *An attempt on a police detective's life results in permanent deafness for the star of this television movie. Gerard then utilizes a speech therapist's services and learns basic communication skills, enabling him to track down drug dealers.
Source: Personal viewing.

67. "The Facts of Life: Sound of Silence" (October 27, 1982). Deaf character: Kim Fields.
Synopsis: Tootie (Fields) has a change of personality and refuses to acknowledge her hearing loss or seek medical help until her friends intervene.

68. "Family Tree" (NBC, January-February 1983), 6 episodes, 60 min., color. Deaf actor: Jonathan Hall Kovacs (a deaf actor).
Synopsis: Based on an earlier television movie (see no. 61), this series featured a deaf child, Toby (Kovacs). Only two episodes deal with deafness per se: in one, the father (Frank Converse) tries to avoid learning sign language (January 29, 1983); in the other, the mother (Anne Archer) is overprotective

of Toby after the house is burgled when he is there alone (February 12, 1983).
Source: *TV Guide*.

69. "Trapper John, M.D.: Hear Today, Gone Tomorrow" (CBS, January 23, 1983), 60 min., color. Director: Vincent Sherman. Producers: Frank Glicksman and Don Brinkley. Script by Jeff Stewart. Deaf character: Madge Sinclair.
Synopsis: *Nurse Ernie Shoop's (Sinclair) pride prevents her from dealing with a hearing loss, until she is nearly struck by an unheard, approaching ambulance. Her condition is diagnosed as otosclerosis, and she has a successful operation. A second story line revolves around music and a disturbed trumpet player.
Source: Film Collection, LC.

70. "T. J. Hooker" (repeated April 23, 1983), 60 min., color. Deaf character: Panchito Gomez.
Synopsis: Hooker (William Shatner) tries to clear a hearing-impaired teenager "who's been left to take a murder rap by his fellow gang members."
Source: *TV Guide*.

71. "St. Elsewhere" (NBC, February 1, 1984), 60 min., color. Director: Charles Braverman. Deaf characters: Bob Daniels, Freda Norman (both deaf actors).
Synopsis: *When emergency room personnel cannot understand a deaf patient (Norman), they call for a hospital employee to interpret. The employee (Daniels) is a deaf radiology technician who has understandable but hearing-impaired speech and can read lips. The episode deals with the difficulties he has with his supervisor, who complains that although Daniels is competent, he is not fast and makes the patients nervous. Dr. Westfall (Ed Flanders) comes to Daniels's aid and tells the supervisor that he must "get used to" his deaf employee. The episode ends with Westfall signing, "See you later."
Source: GU Media 2366.

72. *A Summer to Remember* (CBS, 1984), 120 min., color. Executive Producers: Max Keller and Robert Lewis. Producers: Micheline Keller and Edward Gold. Director: Robert Lewis. Story by Robert Lewis and Scott Swanton. Teleplay by Scott Swanton. Deaf character: Sean Justis Gerlis.
Synopsis: *An unhappy deaf boy, Toby (Gerlis), befriends an escaped orangutan, K.C., who has been taught during an experimental research project to communicate through signs. The boy's mother (Tess Harper) and stepfather (James Farentino) refuse to believe his claim that he has seen a "gorilla," so he and his younger sister (Bridgette Anderson) let K.C. live in their treehouse. Eventually the police capture the orangutan and give him to an abusive circus owner, who places K.C. in a cage with a dying gorilla. Toby and his sister rescue their friend, who is ultimately returned to the research director (Louise Fletcher, the daughter of deaf parents). K.C. tells them in signs that the gorilla is sick, and the authorities take the animal away from the circus

owner. All of the family members use Manual English with Toby, who refuses to talk (a subplot is the effort to get Toby to use his voice). In a climactic scene, however, Toby calls to his friend the orangutan, "K.C., K.C., please come," in his speech-impaired voice.
Source: GU Media 2481.

73. "Fame" (CBS, May 12, 1984), 60 min., color. Deaf characters: Jackie Kinner (a deaf actress), Billy Hufsey.
Synopsis: Chris (Hufsey) must transfer to a school for the deaf when he loses his hearing in an accident. A deaf student, Theresa (Kinner), helps with the transition.
Source: *TV Guide;* personal interview with Jackie Kinner, September 17, 1987.

74. *Johnny Belinda* (CBS, August 31, 1984), 120 min., color. Producer: Stanley Bass. Director: Anthony Page. Teleplay by Sue Milburn. Deaf characters: Rosanna Arquette, Julianna Fjeld (a deaf actress).
Synopsis: *Based on the stage play and film of the 1940s (see no. 30), this version does not tamper with the basic story of a young, illiterate deaf woman (Arquette) whose life is enriched by a young man (Richard Thomas) who teaches her to communicate through signs and finger spelling. Unlike the original film, in this version Belinda has a voice, and although she cannot speak, she does make noise to get attention and also screams when she is raped and later when her son is born. Fjeld appears as a deaf x-ray technician who finger spells a brief message. The communication level is appropriate for two characters who are new to signs and finger spelling.
Source: GU Media 2368.

75. *Helen Keller, the Miracle Continues* (1984), 120 min., color. Producer: Castle Combs Productions. Executive Producer: David Lawrence. Director: Alan Gibson. Teleplay by John McGreevey, based on *Helen and Teacher* by Joseph Lash. Deaf-blind character: Mare Winningham.
Synopsis: *This is the story of Helen Keller (Winningham) as a young adult, focusing on the close relationship of Keller and her teacher, Anne Sullivan (Blythe Danner). John Macy, who is hired to edit Keller's writing, eventually marries Sullivan; however, he is frustrated in his efforts to find a place in the relationship with Keller, and the marriage ends in divorce. Keller, too, seeks a mate, but her plans to elope with Peter Fagan are halted by Sullivan, who dissuades the young suitor from a life as full-time aide to the famous but dependent Keller. Faced with the reality that neither of them will find an outside companion, the two women proceed to earn a living with appearances on the vaudeville stage. Keller speaks in an impaired voice and is reluctant to use it in the presence of strangers. Although finger spelling into the hand is a primary mode of communication throughout this television movie, one never sees clear letters expressed by any of the actors.
Source: GU Media 2362.

76. "Gimme a Break" (NBC, February 1985), 30 min., color. Deaf character: Phyllis Frelich (a deaf actress).
Synopsis: Series star Nell Carter and a deaf woman (Frelich) are temporarily trapped in a library basement during an earthquake. Frelich's character is Hispanic and does not understand English; hence, she cannot lip-read or write notes. Carter does not know sign language. The story focuses on their efforts to learn how to communicate.

77. "The Nanny" (PBS, September 15, 1985), 60 min., color. Deaf character: unknown.
Synopsis: The nanny believes that the child she cares for has a hearing problem, but the parents refuse to accept her opinion.

78. "Alfred Hitchcock Presents" (CBS, December 8, 1985), 30 min., color. Deaf character: Christina Raines.
Synopsis: This remake of a 1956 Hitchcock program features a convict (Yaphet Kotto) who is surprised to learn that his victim is deaf (see TV no. 11).

79. "Hallmark Hall of Fame: Love Is Never Silent" (NBC, December 9, 1985), 120 min., color. Executive producers: Julianna Fjeld and Marian Rees. Director: Joseph Sargent. Technical adviser and ASL consultant: Lou Fant. Based on Joanne Greenberg's novel *In This Sign*. Deaf characters: Phyllis Frelich, Ed Waterstreet, Julianna Fjeld (all deaf actors).
Synopsis: *This teleplay depicts the life of a deaf couple, Janice and Able Ryder (Frelich and Waterstreet), and their hearing daughter, Margaret (Mare Winningham). The focus is on Margaret as the deaf couple's link to the hearing world. Julianna Fjeld appears as the mother's deaf friend and a factory co-worker. Lou Fant (the son of deaf parents) appears as minister of a deaf congregation. The signed communication is excellent, and the audience is able to follow the dialogue through appropriate responses and occasional interpreting by the characters who can hear.
Source: Personal viewing.

80. "The Jeffersons" (1985). Producer: Embassy TV. Deaf character: Jackie Kinner (a deaf actress).
Synopsis: Louise Jefferson participates in a fund-raising effort for disabled children, which includes a mime performance by Kinner.
Source: Personal interview with Jackie Kinner, September 17, 1987.

81. "Spenser for Hire: Silence Speaks" (ABC, February 11, 1986), 60 min., color. Executive producer: John Wilder. Director: Ray Austin. Script by Robert Hamilton. Deaf character: Phyllis Frelich (a deaf actress).
Synopsis: *A deaf newspaperwoman (Frelich) writes an "Uncle Fred" advice column for men. When one of her correspondents, Tyrone, asks for advice when his fiancée pressures him to commit an immoral act, Frelich advises him not to do it. Eventually, Tyrone and "Fred" agree to meet, and when Tyrone does not appear, Frelich hires Spenser (Robert Urich) to find him.

Spenser's mistress, Susan (Barbara Stock), knows sign language and serves as Frelich's interpreter; Spenser uses gestures and speaks slowly when he and "Fred" are alone, and she responds with typed replies on her computer terminal. The mysterious Tyrone is eventually found, and the episode ends when the couple finally meet.
Source: Personal viewing.

82. "Dallas" (CBS, initial appearance in 1986), 60 min., color. Deaf character: Solomon Smaniotto (a deaf actor and a student at the California School for the Deaf in Riverside).
Synopsis: *Donna Krebbs (Susan Howard) loses her baby and to ease the pain volunteers at a school for handicapped children. There she meets Tony (Smaniotto), who is hearing-impaired, and becomes attached to him. The adults' signs and finger spelling are terrible, and the episodes are flawed by a hearing person's perspective that a young deaf boy would want to be adopted by hearing persons, even if they barely can communicate with him.

83. "CBS Schoolbreak Special: Have You Tried Talking to Patty?" (CBS, 1986), 60 min., color. Producer: Diane Asselin. Director: Donald Petrie. Script by Allan and Judith Gansberg. Technical consultant: David Sladek. Deaf character: Mary Vreeland (a deaf actress).
Synopsis: *A deaf student who is mainstreamed into a hearing school is left behind by her two girlfriends, who go off with some young men. Patty (Vreeland) who has a high-pitched voice, signs and finger spells, and reads lips, joins the wrong crowd in an effort to be popular and obtain dates. Her new friends make no effort to sign or finger spell, and they abandon her after shoplifting. She is caught, but one of her schoolmates, a young man who works at the store and was previously frustrated in his efforts to communicate with her, prevails with the shopowner to let Patty go. Having learned her lesson, Patty returns to her old friends. The story ends with Patty at the school dance. The depiction of communication (signed English) and technology, such as flashing lights and telecommunication devices, is accurate.
Source: GU Media (no assigned number).

84. "Magnum, P.I.: One Picture Is Worth" (CBS, October 8, 1986), 60 min., color. Executive producers: Charles F. Johnson and Chris Abbott-Fish. Producers: Jay Huguely and Rick Weaver. Director: Ray Austin. Script by James L. Novack. Deaf character: Stephanie Dunnam.
Synopsis: *A deaf woman who lost her hearing five years ago witnesses a bank robbery and the subsequent murder of four other witnesses. Magnum (Tom Selleck), who is assigned to protect her, takes her to the estate where he lives. Higgins (John Hillerman) informs Magnum that Linda, the witness, is an internationally acclaimed primitive artist. Although Linda speaks naturally and lip-reads very well, Higgins uses some signs with her; the execution of both signs and finger spelling is poor and serves no useful purpose in the

story. Eventually, the bank robbers discover Linda's identity and trap her at her isolated art studio to which she has fled. Magnum comes to her rescue and, while fending off the attack, Linda uses a pair of binoculars to read the villains' lips and apprise Magnum of their movements.
Source: Personal viewing.

85. "Airwolf" (1986). Producer: Universal TV. Deaf character: Jackie Kinner (a deaf actress).
Synopsis: A member of the Airwolf team, Katie, attends her class reunion and is held hostage by terrorists who have kidnapped one of the wealthy classmates. Kinner plays a pregnant and deaf classmate who is also held hostage.
Source: Personal interview with Jackie Kinner, September 17, 1987.

86. "Cagney & Lacey" (CBS, March 9, 1987), 60 min., color. Producers: Barney Rosenzweig, Georgia Jeffries, and Ralph Singleton. Director: Sharon Miller. Teleplay by David Abramowitz. Story by Becky Cole and David Abramowitz. Deaf character: Terrylene Theriot.
Synopsis: *Cagney (Sharon Gless) and Lacey (Tyne Daly) confront a deaf teenager, Michelle Bennet (Theriot), who is holding a gun and standing over a dead drug dealer. Lacey is upset that she almost shot Bennet, who failed to hear her command to drop the gun. Claiming self-defense, Bennet uses her deafness to gain sympathy and eventually is released, since the lieutenant (Al Waxman) and the prosecutor do not wish to be accused of harassing a deaf suspect. From another witness Cagney and Lacey discover that someone else with a history of preying on drug dealers was at the murder scene. Bennet denies this, but shortly after her release, that other person is found dead. Lacey realizes that Bennet was lying and rearrests her. In the subsequent interrogation, Bennet drops her mask of innocence and demands an attorney. The signing is authentic; and audiences understand what transpires through the presence of an interpreter, Helen Grovner (Michelle Baron), who also explains that Bennet is ill educated and uses primitive signs. This is a rare example of a deaf villain in television programming.
Source: Personal viewing.

Sign-Language Motion Pictures for the Deaf Community

The disabled community in general, and hearing-impaired persons in particular, historically have overestimated their numbers. Even today, many publications routinely refer to fourteen to twenty million hearing-impaired persons in the United States whenever they wish to justify the need for governmental services or assistive devices such as decoders for captioned television. The reality of the market is much lower, and Hollywood understood this when it chose to ignore the requests of both deaf and hard-of-hearing patrons in 1929 to continue showing silent, captioned films. Although it is true that a large number of Americans have some sort of hearing impairment, profound deafness remains a low-incidence disability and, as such, has never commanded, and probably never will, the attention of major film producers and distributors.

A few enterprising deaf individuals have tried to fill the entertainment vacuum for the deaf community. In addition to the film project of the National Association of the Deaf, sign-language films were produced in California, Ohio, and New York. Contemporary reports of these films indicate that they made use of deaf actors and that they were designed to be shown in deaf club settings, often accompanied by live entertainment, usually the individual who produced the film or members of the cast.

Compared to the number of films produced by the black and Hispanic communities, "deaf" films are few in number; however, with some exceptions most of them remain available through the Gallaudet University Archives and the media collection. Here I identify those "entertainment" films that have been shown routinely at deaf community events and were designed specifically for deaf patrons. The Gallaudet collection also contains films and videotapes of other relevant materials, such as filmed performances of college theater groups, which include many of the deaf actors who work in television today. For further details, readers should consult the *Gallaudet Media Distribution Service Catalogue* (Washington, D.C., 1982). Many of the National Association of the Deaf films are available at the Motion Picture Division of the Library of Congress. The originals were 35mm, nitrate-based film, but in the 1940s the NAD arranged to convert them to 16mm safety-film and gave copies to the Library of Congress and to Gallaudet College (which acquired university status in the fall of 1986). Since the spring of 1985, Gallaudet has published *Deaf Mosaic,* the nation's only broadcast magazine/program for and about deaf people. Distributed monthly by PBS stations and the Discovery Channel, *Deaf Mosaic* features stories about the deaf community, including film and television coverage. Interested readers should contact the Television Department at Gallaudet for a press kit and list of feature stories.

1. *The Lorna Doone Country of Devonshire, England* (NAD, 1910), 12 min., 16mm, b&w, silent.
Synopsis: *The NAD claims that this was the first signed lecture on film; however, see the description of film no. 1, *Deaf Mute Girl Reciting "Star Spangled Banner"* (1902) for an earlier example of filmed sign language. In this film the college's first president, Edward Miner Gallaudet, recites the story of Lorna Doone and tells of a visit to the area.
Source: GU Media 99.

2. *The Discovery of Chloroform* (NAD, 1913), 8 min., 16mm, b&w, silent.

Synopsis: *The first chairman of the NAD's Moving Picture committee, Oscar H. Regensberg, introduces this film in which George T. Dougherty, deaf leader and chemist, describes the discovery of chloroform.
Source: GU Media 108.

3. *An Address at the Tomb of Garfield* (NAD, 1913), 9 min., 16mm, b&w, silent.
Synopsis: *In a memorial service, Willis Hubbard, an NAD leader and a Michigan teacher, describes the life of the assassinated president James A. Garfield and his interest in Gallaudet College. Since the college depends upon a federal subsidy, its officers and the deaf community have long cultivated the friendship of national politicians such as Garfield.
Source: GU Media 107.

4. *Death of Minnehaha* (NAD, 1913), 16 min., 16mm, b&w, silent.
Synopsis: *A Michigan teacher of the deaf, Mary W. Erd, recites Longfellow's famous poem, in costume. Erd is the only female signer to appear in the NAD films.
Source: GU Media 106.

5. *Dom Pedro's Visit to Gallaudet College* (NAD, 1913), 6 min., 16mm, b&w, silent.
Synopsis: *Edward A. Fay, a Gallaudet College vice president and faculty member, describes a visit to the college by the emperor of Brazil in 1876.
Source: GU Media 100.

6. *The Irishman's Flea* and *The Lady and the Cake* (NAD, 1913), 3 min., 16mm, b&w, silent.
Synopsis: *Robert McGregor recites two contemporary examples of platform humor designed for deaf audiences.
Source: GU Archives 115.

7. *A Lay Sermon: The Universal Brotherhood and Fatherhood of God* (NAD, 1913), 16 min., 16mm, b&w, silent.
Synopsis: *Robert McGregor presents a sermon for deaf audiences.
Source: GU Media 104.

8. *Memories of Old Hartford* (NAD, 1913), 16 min., 16mm, b&w, silent.
Synopsis: *John B. Hotchkiss, a Gallaudet faculty member, describes his student days at the first school for the deaf in the United States, located in Hartford, Connecticut.
Source: GU Media 101.

9. *Preservation of the Sign Language* (NAD, 1913), 16 min., 16mm, b&w, silent.
Synopsis: *The seventh president of the NAD, George Veditz, asks for funds from the deaf community to preserve sign language on motion picture film. This particular film remains at the heart of the NAD collection. Although the

original film was not captioned, Gallaudet College has captioned this footage for persons unfamiliar with sign language.
Source: GU Media 105.

10. *Gettysburg* (NAD, 1915), 12 min., 16mm, b&w, silent.
Synopsis: *A prominent deaf minister, A. D. Bryant, describes and guides the audience across the Gettysburg battlefield.
Source: GU Media 103.

11. *The Signing of the Charter of Gallaudet College* (NAD, 1915), 15 min., 16mm, b&w, silent.
Synopsis: *Amos G. Draper, a Gallaudet faculty member, describes the signing of the college charter by Abraham Lincoln in 1864.
Source: GU Media 102.

12. *A Chapter from the Life of Thomas Hopkins Gallaudet* (NAD, 1920), 6 min., 16mm, b&w, silent.
Synopsis: *This is a scene from an unfinished play about Thomas Hopkins Gallaudet in which his son, Edward, discusses the future with his parents.
Source: GU Media 110.

13. *Yankee Doodle* (NAD, 1920), 6 min., 16mm, b&w, silent.
Synopsis: *Winfield Marshall, a storyteller, performs the popular song, in costume.
Source: GU Media 111.

14. *The Selfish Mr. Tiggnty* (M.C. Movie Production Company, Akron, Ohio, 1930s).
Synopsis: Obsessed with efficiency, Mr. Tiggnty replaces his employees with robots. When the robots burn out because of overwork, Tiggnty goes bankrupt, but wakes up to discover it was only a bad dream. This same deaf movie company planned another film, *The Headless Revenge,* but it is not known whether this second film was completed. Akron, Ohio, was the locale of a sizable deaf community because tire manufacturers were among the early large-scale employers of deaf workers.
Source: Film has not been found.

15. *Dog Trouble* (ca. 1945).
Synopsis: Promoted as the "first deaf full-length color production," advertisements for this film, produced in California, appeared in the *Silent Cavalier* in the fall of 1945, along with a schedule of showings at deaf clubs throughout the United States. Club presentations included a short film about *Deaf Workers in War Plants* and personal appearances by some members of the film's cast: Teresa Cikoch, Chester Beers, and Albert Mangan.
Source: Film has not been found.

16. *Silent Symphony* (1954), 12 min., 16mm, color, silent.
Synopsis: *This is a filmed sign-mime performance by a deaf entertainer,

Bernard Bragg, at the Greek Theatre in Berkeley, California. Bragg performs a skit in which he is both the director and the entire cast.

Source: GU Media 143.

17. *The Debt* (Independent Theatrical and Cinema Club for the Deaf, 1955), 65 min., 3/4-inch videotape, b&w, silent. Director: Ernest Marshall. Script by Ernest Marshall and LeRoy R. Subit. Adapted from the play by Anton Chekhov.

Synopsis: *One of several films produced with an all-deaf cast from the New York City area. Ernest Marshall viewed the silent film actor Emerson Romero as his mentor. Romero advised the deaf filmmaker to always look for a good story.

Source: GU Archives 2681. Marshall retains personal possession of all the films produced by the Cinema Club but has provided videotaped copies to Gallaudet University for limited use on campus. Ernest Marshall to John Schuchman, Videotaped Interview, October 1981, GU Archives.

18. *Oedipus Rex* (Gallaudet, 1957), 20 min., 16mm, color, silent.

Synopsis: *This is a college dramatic club presentation of an adaptation of Sophocles's play, made available to the national deaf community. See a filmed interview with the play's director, George Detmold, for a discussion of how sound tapes were used with the signing of the deaf actors (GU Archives 175). For other films produced by Gallaudet College, see the media catalog.

Source: GU Media 33.

19. *The Dream* (aka *Ten Barrooms in One Night*) (Independent Theatrical and Cinema Club for the Deaf, 1961), 30 min., 3/4-inch videotape, b&w, silent. Director: Ernest Marshall.

Synopsis: *Based on the melodrama *Ten Barrooms in One Night*, this is the story of a deaf man who falls asleep and dreams about a tavern and its patrons. The producers provided captions for the signed dialogue.

Source: GU Archives 2554.

20. *Ernest Marshall Films* (Independent Theatrical and Cinema Club for the Deaf, 1937–63), 120 min., 3/4-inch videotape, b&w, silent.

Synopsis: *This videotape includes the following films:

a. *Cyrano de Bergerac* (ca. 1937): filmed rehearsals of a play performed at St. Anne's Church for the Deaf in New York.

b. *The Magic of Magicians* (ca. 1938). Director: Ernest Marshall.

c. *I Knew Hereafter* (n.d.)

d. *The Confession* (ca. 1956). Director: Ernest Marshall.

e. *The Neighbor* (ca. 1961). Director: Ernest Marshall.

f. *Sorrowful Approach* (ca. 1962). Director: Kathleen Fettin.

g. *A Cake of Soap* (ca. 1963). Director: Emerson Romero (a former silent film actor).

Source: GU Archives 2685.

21. *Moses* (Joyce Motion Pictures, 1973), 45 min., 16mm, color, sound.
Synopsis: Lou Fant (the son of deaf parents) tells the biblical story of Moses.
For further information on Joyce films, see the Gallaudet media catalog or
contact the film company, located in Los Angeles, California.
Source: GU Media 198.

22. *Deafula* (Signscope, 1975), 95 min., color, sound. Director: Peter
Wechsberg. Producer: Garry Holstrom. Script by Peter Wechsberg.
Synopsis: This sign-language film utilizes the familiar Dracula story as a
springboard for a description of "the frustration, and sometimes, horror of
the deaf world."
Source: Signscope Inc. (Ventura, Calif.). Gallaudet College has in its possession an interview with Wechsberg in which he discusses the film; however,
the complete film is not available.

23. *Jabberwocky* (Joyce Motion Pictures, 1975), 10 min., 16mm, color,
sound.
Synopsis: Lewis Carroll's poem is signed by Lou Fant (the son of deaf
parents).
Source: GU Media 191.

24. *The Legend of Old Bill* (Joyce Motion Pictures, 1975), 9 min., 16mm,
color, silent.
Synopsis: Willard Madsen, a Gallaudet faculty member and sign-language
teacher, tells the story of a hermit.
Source: GU Media 183.

25. *My Motor's Missing* (Joyce Motion Pictures, 1975), 3 min., 16mm,
color, silent.
Synopsis: This brief comedy is about a deaf woman who misunderstands the
message of a gas station attendent.
Source: GU Media 187.

26. *The Necklace* (Joyce Motion Pictures, 1975), 20 min., 16mm, color,
silent.
Synopsis: Ralph White, a deaf teacher and actor, narrates this mystery.
Source: GU Media 189.

27. *Think Me Nothing* (rel. Signscope, 1979), 127 min., color, sound.
Producer and director: David Jarashow.
Synopsis: The drug and sex adventures of a young deaf man and his friends
in southern California are portrayed. Characters use signs, with a voice-over
for hearing audiences.
Source: Signscope, Inc. (Ventura, Calif.).

Name and Subject Index

Title Index

UNIVERSITY OF ILLINOIS PRESS
1325 SOUTH OAK STREET
CHAMPAIGN, ILLINOIS 61820-6903
WWW.PRESS.UILLINOIS.EDU